SCALE AIRCRAFT for FREE FLIGHT

Eric Coates on
SCALE AIRCRAFT for FREE FLIGHT
Edited by Vic Smeed

Nexus Special Interests

Nexus Special Interests Ltd.
Nexus House
Boundary Way
Hemel Hempstead
Herts HP2 7ST
England

First published in this book form 1998

© Nexus Special Interests Ltd. 1998

ISBN 1-85486-167-0

All rights reserved. No part of this publication may be reproduced in any form, by print, photography, microfilm or any other means without written permission from the publisher.

Phototypesetting by The Studio, Exeter

Printed and bound in Great Britain by
Marston Book Services Limited, Oxfordshire

Contents

	Preface	6
CHAPTER 1	**Introduction**	8
CHAPTER 2	**Selection of Prototype** *The effect of the gyrocouple and torque.* *Some suggested prototypes.*	14
CHAPTER 3	**Design Features**	26
CHAPTER 4	**Fuselage Construction** *Undercarriages. Cabanes.*	35
CHAPTER 5	**Rigging and Wing Attachment**	46
CHAPTER 6	**Wing and Tailplane Construction** *Wing structure.*	56
CHAPTER 7	**Covering and Finishing** *Applying the finish.*	67
CHAPTER 8	**Detail** *Propellers. Cowls. Engine details. Cockpits.* *Pilots. Guns. Undercarriages. Wheels. Fabric lacing.*	79
CHAPTER 9	**Flying** *Pre-flight checks. Initial test glides. Power trimming.* *Final trimming flights. Contest flying*	101
	Glossary	125

Preface

One of the most revered names in the field of free-flying scale models is that of Eric Coates, who died in the early 1990s. For many years no event for this type of model was complete without his presence; he was a successful competitor and a pathfinder in the development of greater scale accuracy. The series of articles written by him which appeared in *Aeromodeller* in 1971/72 remains a leading source of practical advice on how to go about designing, building and flying a scale model and it is upon this series that this book is based.

Although he did fly radio models, the challenge of making consistent, stable and safe flights with an accurate scale machine without in-flight control is what really appealed to Eric. Fellow contestants tended to pull his leg about always choosing reasonably safe prototypes, but his long experience indicated that the lightly loaded, slow flying aircraft of the early days of aviation – perhaps particularly World War I biplanes – offered the best vehicles in which to put the hours of meticulous work which typified his models. Later prototypes, especially fast monoplanes, are far more suited to radio control, but many modellers who started the hobby when rubber was king find that radio flying lacks something; once you can fly a radio model every flight is likely to be similar whereas wind, weather and terrain cause variations in free flight and introduce the possible element of the unexpected, even, at times, a degree of apprehension regarding possible loss or damage. Both types of modelling make the same demands in construction and, perhaps, trimming, but thereafter the free-flying machine offers more of a risk factor, which many fliers find addictive.

Be that as it may, Eric wrote about his favoured types of model and most of what he set down is as valid today as it was when first published. There have been developments in adhesives and covering materials, in particular, and standards of accuracy and construction have risen, but a model built

PREFACE

according to the methods set out in this book would, with care and patience, still compete with the best at national level. Editing the series into book form has provided the opportunity of substituting current products for any which have ceased to be available and allowed a small amount of updating, all minimum amendments which are believed to be in line with the Coates philosophy. As far as possible the original illustrations have been reproduced; many of these show the author's friends and fellow competitors with models which, though flying around thirty years ago, would be exactly the same if built today.

Vic Smeed
January 1998

Eric Coates (right) at a scale meeting at Old Warden in 1972, discussing with J. G. Watkins the difficulty of persuading his Bristol Type D Scout to take off – something which appears characteristic of this design.

CHAPTER 1

Introduction

The free-flight scale model seemed to lose popularity, at least with the more serious modeller, in the 1960s and 70s, being, no doubt, a reflection on the increasing popularity of the radio model. Entries in the SMAE Super Scale event for free-flight scale models during the period declined almost in an inverse ratio to the increase in entries for the Radio Control Scale event. There are many well-known fliers of radio-controlled scale models today who have never flown a free-flight scale job. This is a pity, for many as the delights are in flying radio there is charm, which all who practise the art will endorse, in operating a lightly loaded free-flight scale model on calm evenings which, in my opinion, surpasses all other forms of model flying. This charm seems to be enhanced if the subject is a biplane, a type in which I have specialised for over 20 years.

Undoubtedly biplanes, particularly machines of the 1914–18 period with their generous area, are the most suitable subjects for free flight, most of them being relatively easily trimmed. Full realism of flight never seems to be captured if these aeroplanes are produced as radio-controlled models and much less so as control-line models. The added weight of the radio-control gear increases the wing loading and the use of powerful motors to provide the necessary penetration for contest flying on all but the calmest days usually destroys the innate flying characteristics of the prototype. The necessity to fly

The Miles Hawk built by me in 1953 is typical of the more difficult type of model to trim, due to its low wing layout etc., and was always rather nerve-racking to fly.

INTRODUCTION

My most successful model, contest-wise, was this Bucker Jüngmann, built in 1966, and still a regular performer five years on. It won the Super Scale trophy in 1967.

at speeds in excess of scale, to maintain line tension, and the unbanked turn of the control-line model are also completely alien to the vintage biplane.

The intention is not to decry radio-controlled and control-line scale models, but just to show that certain types are better suited to be modelled as free-flight subjects. Without doubt the low-wing fighter of World War II is best suited as a radio-controlled model and the multi-engined bomber is best flown on lines. Conversely the more difficult types can be made to fly free flight but these machines are much more troublesome to trim and with the worry of a prang always present the 'charm' is not so much in evidence.

I first became interested in building free-flight scale models immediately after the Second World War when the 'solid scale' boom of the war years was over. Most of my early scale models were built from the multitude of small rubber scale kits then offered by the many British kit manufacturers. The kits of those days seemed to offer far greater value than those proffered today, and generally being of much lighter construction put in far better performances than is possible from some of today's heavyweight kit models. This is a pity, for the small scale rubber kit is a common introduction to modelling for youngsters, and if it doesn't fly another potential aeromodeller is lost.

The 44in. span Avro 504 K, built over 40 years ago, weighed a mere $13\frac{1}{2}$oz and flew originally on a .5cc diesel. I have never since managed to build a model with such a light wing loading!

SCALE AIRCRAFT FOR FREE FLIGHT

This fine action shot of Terry Manley's Bristol Scout Type D ideally illustrates the appeal of the 'bipe'.

The natural progression from these models was, in the 1940s, to the larger rubber scale models and it is in this branch I must confess to almost total failure! Many were the scale rubber designs published in the *Aeromodeller* of those days by such names as E. J. Riding (tragically killed in an air accident in 1949), J. M. Greenland and C. Rupert Moore etc.; the latter gentleman even patented a device called the 'Moore Diaphragm', to keep the majority of the rubber at the forward end of the fuselage and so prevent the CG moving too far aft – a particular curse of the short-nosed biplane, even now with all the weight of the power unit concentrated forward. Although I built several of the designs of these revered gentlemen, success eluded me as I am afraid my models were invariably too heavy for the limited power available and a long drawn out power glide was usually the best which they could manage. I therefore became disillusioned with the free-flight rubber scale model and, like many other modellers in the late 1940s, was swept up with the control-line boom. My interest soon turned to scale again and now with plenty of power available from the Mills, EDs and Elfins of those days many were the World War I biplanes to be seen flying on the end of my wires. Admittedly these were appalling creations, by the standards of today, but, as their life was usually short, this was of small consequence compared to the rapidity of building. Two or three weeks at the most was sufficient for a scale model in those days for me!

With the advent of the Amco 0.87cc diesel in 1948, followed shortly after by the Mills 0.75cc, the whole world of scale modelling was changed. Here

INTRODUCTION

at last were reliable power units no more than 2in. high and weighing only 2oz or so, which could lift a model weighing over a pound, and around 40in. span, with ease. Indeed, the Mills .75 has never been improved upon as the ideal scale power unit. Easy starting, easy to cowl, due to the rear induction, and the ability to swing props up to 10in. diameter made it a natural. Production of this engine, and of other similar long-stroke motors, ceased when fashion dictated a change to front induction short-stroke designs which revved like the devil on a 5in. prop which wouldn't clear the cowling diameter and protested and died if shown anything over 8in. diameter. Fortunately the Mills became available again, originally from Indian sources but later once again made in England, to be followed by several other 'revivals' of engines suitable for scale models.

Being well and truly hooked on control-line models when these engines were first introduced, it was some time before I realised what potential they offered for free-flight scale. There was a widely held view at that time that it was a far more difficult task to fly power scale than rubber scale, and it was not until I saw a fellow member of the old Goole and DMS flying a converted APS rubber-powered Tiger Moth powered by a 1cc ED Bee that the penny dropped. Almost overnight the control-line handle was discarded and I was designing the first of a long line of powered free-flight scale models, stretching over some forty years.

My first successful powered design was the dear old Avro 504 K built in 1950. My aim in this model was to produce as light a machine as possible to fly on very low power. It was fitted with one of the first Allbon .5cc Darts and the all-up weight was only $13\frac{1}{2}$ oz. This for a 44in. span model was quite

Terry Manley releases his beautiful Hannover CL 111a in the 1967 Super Scale event, held at RAF Upwood, where it took second place.

Compare this picture of my BE 12d with the Avro 504 K on page 9 to contrast the difference in 20 years of building. Scale accuracy is now far superior to the 'old days' when areas and outlines were frequently altered to increase the flying ability.

remarkable for me and I have never managed to produce anything with such a light wing loading again. Unfortunately, the drag was too much for the Dart, which is not an ideal scale motor, and it had to be re-engined with one of the early ED 1cc Bees. This combination was perfect. The old 504 lumbered around the small fields surrounding Goole for nearly two years. She flew so slowly that when she hit anything, which was quite frequently, damage was minimal or non-existent. By present-day standards the scale accuracy and finish (red Modelspan was used for the covering) must have been appalling, nevertheless, the old Avro was the biggest milestone in my aeromodelling career and probably gave me more pleasure than anything else I have built, including multi-channel radio-controlled models in later years.

Between the Avro and the BE illustrated lay 20 years of continuous development in construction techniques not only by me, but by many other leading scale modellers, notably Bridgewood, Simmance and Manley, whose ideas have been freely 'cribbed' and incorporated into succeeding models. Some have found to be wanting and rejected on the next model but over the years, the technique has slowly evolved. This, together with improvements in materials, adhesives (the coming of epoxies and the ability to bond wire and wood together in a satisfactory manner being possibly the greatest improvement of all) and trimming methods, means that today you can confidently

A long-lived model, that finally met an ignominious end when it was crushed during a house removal, was my Sopwith $1\frac{1}{2}$ Strutter which often used to 'formate' with Terry Manley's Scout D.

INTRODUCTION

build a realistic looking aeroplane that will fly well, even in quite windy conditions without too great a risk of damaging them. Nowadays most of my models average a five-year flying life. During their first two years I limit their flying to preserve their appearance for contests, but after that they are used as sport models and fly most weekends and summer evenings when the weather is reasonable. I still possess, in flying order, the Jüngmann which was built in 1966, and which had more contest successes for me than anything else I have produced. Apart from winning the Super Scale event in 1966, it won three other events and had several other placings. The relatively heavy wing loading and stability provided by the 11-degree sweepback of the wings made it a safe performer even in half a gale.

The longest lived of all my models was the $1\frac{1}{2}$ Strutter, which was built in 1959 and finally ended its days by being crushed in my move to the south of England in 1967. During the mid 1960s a regular sight on Brough Airfield was to see the $1\frac{1}{2}$ and the Scout D of Terry Manley formating together. They both possessed almost identical flight patterns and if launched simultaneously would follow one another round in circles for minutes on end on a calm evening. On only two occasions did they collide and then the damage was only slight. Of course, like old soldiers, good models must die sometime. If you are careful with the trimming this should be only after several years' service when the ravishes of diesel fuel seriously weaken the structure and you are presented with a pile of wreckage.

All the preceding may be rather a personal reminiscence but I hope it portrays something of the joys of building and flying free-flight models. In succeeding chapters I hope to cover, in some detail, all facets of design, construction and flying of free-flight scale models, from the selection of suitable prototypes through structure, covering and finish to detail parts such as engines, wheels, guns etc. A separate chapter will be devoted to rigging and wing fixing which often causes the greatest problems to novices in scale modelling. We shall then carry on to test flights, trimming, and general advice on both sport and competition flying.

It is hoped that these notes will kindle interest in this fascinating branch of aeromodelling and set some of the new generation of modellers along as enjoyable a path as I travelled for many years.

CHAPTER 2

Selection of Prototype

Fifty years ago the literature available on aeroplanes was only a minute fraction of that available today. The data available to the aeromodeller, from which to choose a suitable prototype for a flying scale model, usually consisted of 1/72nd scale drawings of dubious accuracy and what photographs one could lay one's hands on. Information on 1914–18 types was particularly scanty. The museums and collections were nothing like as extensive in their stocks of aeroplanes either, so it was difficult or impossible to view and photograph for oneself a chosen subject. Today, the situation is vastly different. Apart from the multitude of excellent reference books on aeroplanes, containing many superb photographs and coloured plates, the number of aeroplanes on general view to the public in this country is considerable – the best places to view aeroplanes being the Imperial War Museum, especially at Duxford, the Science Museum in London, the Shuttleworth Collection at Old Warden near Biggleswade, the Naval Air Museum at Yeovilton and of course the RAF Museum at Hendon. There are also many smaller museums, often with a dozen or more interesting aircraft.

Another of my models was the Miles Hawk of just 22in. span. Its weight was only 6oz despite being all-sheet covered.

---SELECTION OF PROTOTYPE---

My SE 5a, built in 1968. A low thrust line such as this aircraft possesses requires some downthrust to bring the thrust line above the CG.

In addition, many vintage machines are in private ownership, or in the custody of the various aircraft manufacturers. Usually, such machines can be viewed and photographed by special permission of the owner who is generally only too pleased to co-operate. Extra data, particularly on markings and sub type, can be obtained through perusal of the records of the Imperial War Museum photographic library. I have found the personnel there particularly helpful when I was researching data for my BE 12b, a little known defence fighter derivative of the BE 2c. Unfortunately, the library may only be viewed, by appointment, on Tuesdays to Fridays, 10am to 5pm.

The standard of scale contests, particularly in radio control, has now risen so high that it is imperative that a comprehensive set of photographs and dimensions of the scale subject is obtained to produce an accurate reproduction. These can only be obtained by visiting the original or diligent research amongst the archives. For the average aeromodeller, however, a good general arrangement (GA) drawing and two or three photographs or a 'Profile' should suffice. A word of warning though, do not take the printed colours to be 'gospel', they are often artist interpretations of what he thinks the colours were on the original and sometimes considerable licence is taken and even then, the printing process alters tones.

With regard to the GA drawing, again beware of some of the originals provided by co-operative PROs of the aircraft manufacturers. These again are very often far from accurate. Aeroplanes were not built from such drawings, they were very often drawn by the most junior of draughtsmen for illustration purposes, but aircraft manufacturers usually have good quality photographs available of their past products. However, usually they are of prototypes and do not show service markings. The best source of suitable GA drawings is (naturally!) the *Aeromodeller*. These are mostly very accurate and available in several scales; usually 1/72in. and 1/48in. A full list of drawings – some 450

Terry Manley's Hannover CL 111a flew well, despite the small tailplane area, although very careful trimming was necessary to avoid causing a stall.

currently – appears in a Scale Drawings catalogue, available from the publishers of this book.

Having covered most sources from which information is available let us now consider the choosing of a suitable aeroplane to model. There is an old aeromodelling saying that even a brick will fly, if you trim it properly! While I won't altogether agree with the statement in its literal sense, there is a considerable amount of truth in it. Virtually all model aeroplanes can be made to fly free flight for a while, but for regular operation a degree of inherent stability is desirable if the model is to fly in anything but a flat calm and land in one piece. As a rider to the 'brick' saying it should be added that a light brick is a darn sight easier to trim than a heavy one! To enlarge – although weight has no relation to stability it has a direct relationship on the flying speed. During the early trimming stages, the model is almost bound to strike the ground at some pretty awkward angles and the slower it does the striking the better. It is very easy when making scale models to get wound up in the weight/strength vicious circle. A certain amount of strength in the structure is needed to withstand the impact, therefore you make the model stronger and heavier, so it hits the ground even harder and requires more strength and so on. It is very difficult to know when to stop. We shall deal with this problem in detail in the chapters on structures (Chapters 4, 5 and 6).

To return to the stability problem, I do not propose to go into the theory of stability in great detail. Many articles have been written on the subject over the years in model publications and any volume on basic aerodynamics will explain all that is required for those interested. However, I think it advantageous that we look at the types of stability we are interested in and point out the desirable attributes in an aeroplane to ensure it possesses sufficient inherent stability to keep itself out of trouble.

(a) Lateral stability

Lateral stability is the stability of the aircraft in the rolling plane, i.e. with the aircraft trying to turn about a line through the fuselage. Both static and aerodynamic forces act upon the aeroplane and affect its inherent lateral stability. The mass of the aircraft can be said to act at its centre of gravity and the summation of all the lift forces act at the centre of lift. For an aeroplane to be laterally stable it is essential that the CL is above the CG. The higher the CL above the CG the more stable will be the aircraft. It can therefore automatically be seen that the parasol machine, i.e. an aeroplane with one high-set wing, such as a Fokker DVIII or a Westland Widgeon, has a very stable layout. Biplanes are generally very good also, particularly if the upper wing is set high. Other factors, too, influence the stability of biplanes. Only if both wings are identical in area and work at the same angle of incidence can the CL be said to act midway between the planes. If, as very often is the case, the upper wing is of larger area than the bottom, or is working at a greater angle of incidence, then the CL will be raised. Similarly the amount of dihedral present will lift the CL. The worst case for lateral stability is the low-wing model and it is for this reason that they are the least popular of all free-flight models. However, it is possible to make a low wing stable. The use of a heavy undercarriage and concentration of the weight in the bottom of the fuselage, coupled with a fair degree of dihedral, can usually get the CL above the CG, but not very far unless an exaggerated amount of dihedral is used, which completely ruins the scale appearance. Low wingers then are generally on the margin of stability and can be expected to have to take a fair amount of punishment. For this reason they should be built light and strong. This invariably means small also, to withstand the punishment they are sure to get. The Miles Hawk illustrated was just 22in. span, all-sheet covered and weighed only 6oz. Powered by an ED .46cc diesel it flew well on power but fell out of the sky when the engine cut. Knock-off wings and the light weight, however, prevented damage.

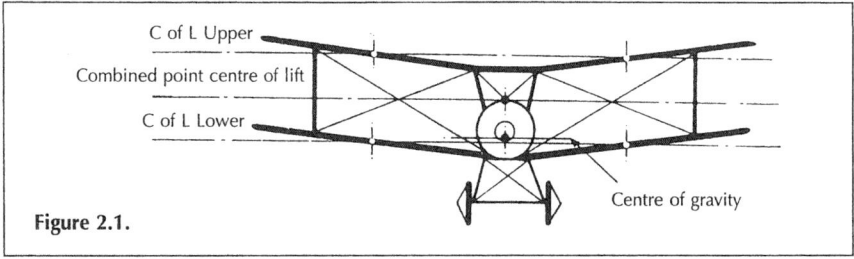

Figure 2.1.

Dihedral has another effect on the stability of an aeroplane apart from raising the centre of lift.

When a gust upsets the attitude of the model, as shown in Fig. 2.2, the weight of the machine will cause it to sideslip, the airflow strikes the undersurface of the lowest wing and the upper surfaces of the highest wing causing a righting couple, to bring the aircraft back to an even keel. The greater the dihedral angle the greater will be the projected area in the slip flow and, therefore, the greater the righting couple.

Sweepback, which also affects directional stability, has an effect on lateral stability also. This is rather difficult to explain but the combination of normal chordwise flow over the wing with the slip flow combines to give a stabilising moment similar to that shown in Fig. 2.2. The effect is not as marked as with

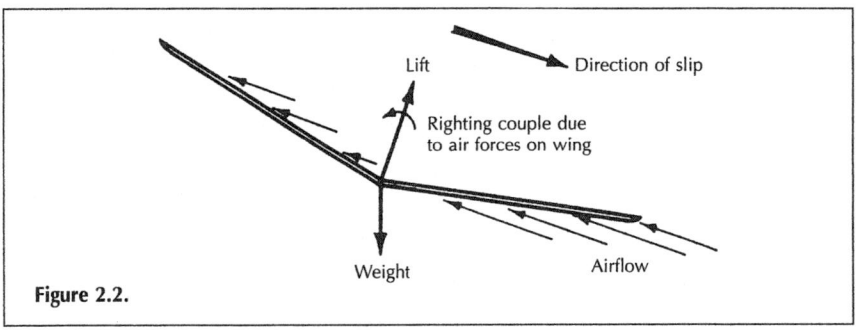

Figure 2.2.

dihedral though. I have found that 3 degrees of sweepback gives approximately the same stability effect as 1 degree of dihedral. When considerable sweepback is present, as in the Jüngmann illustrated previously (11 degrees) then a very stable set-up is assured.

(b) Longitudinal stability

Longitudinal stability is the stability of an aeroplane in the pitching plane, i.e. with the aircraft trying to turn about a line through the centre of gravity, parallel to the wings. Oscillatory motion about this axis is what is generally called stalling. Reference to Fig. 2.3 will show the four major forces acting about this line when the aircraft is in level flight. First we have the weight W acting directly through the centre of gravity and therefore having no movement.

Second, we have drag D acting through the centre of drag, a distance 'd' from the CG. If the centre of drag is above the CG as in Fig. 2.3, the drag will produce a nose-up pitching couple. If the centre of drag is below the CG then the drag will produce a nose-down pitching couple. Generally, high-wing machines and biplanes have their CD above the CG and low-wing machines vice versa.

The third force to consider is the lift L, acting through the centre of lift, a distance 'l' from the CG. If the CL is aft of the CG then the lift will produce a nose-down pitching couple Ll. If the CL is forward of the CG then a nose-up pitching couple will result. The set-up as shown in Fig. 2.3 is a stable one because drag and lift tend to cancel each other out. When you trim for glide by ballasting, either forward or aft, you alter the CG in relation to the CL and

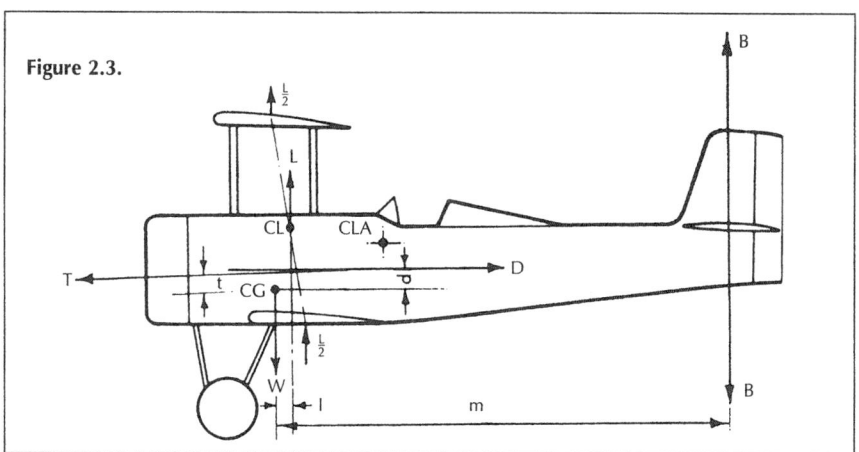

Figure 2.3.

CD so that at the natural gliding speed, i.e. when $W \simeq L$, the forces are in equilibrium.

The fourth force, thrust T, of course, is only present when the engine is running. The thrust line should pass very close to the CG; preferably just above it. Again in the trimming process, adjustment to the thrust line i.e. downthrust or upthrust, may be necessary to maintain our equilibrium of forces when the engine is running. Almost certainly when under power and flying faster than when gliding, the balance of the L and D couples will not be maintained and, therefore, the thrust couple T will have to provide a compensation to maintain equilibrium.

The large fin on my Blackburn Ripon illustrates my point concerning this necessity with long-nosed aircraft.

It can easily be seen that aeroplanes with low thrust lines like the DH 4 or the SE 5a will require a certain amount of downthrust to bring the thrust line above the CG. With an aeroplane like the BAC Drone it is impossible to bring the thrust line near the CG and, therefore, only very low-powered motors can be used in such a position if an unstable pitch-down attitude is to be avoided.

To return to Fig. 2.3 and our balance of force couples about the CG. Everything would be fine as long as the aircraft flew in perfectly smooth air in a straight line. As we all know, such conditions just do not exist and, therefore, some means of stabilisation to keep the whole set-up in equilibrium when disturbing forces affect it is necessary. This is provided by the tailplane. If the aircraft starts to pitch nose-down, air pressure on the top surface of the tailplane produces a force B, acting in a downward direction through the centre of pressure of the tailplane, a distance M from the CG. Similarly, when the aircraft pitches nose-up, a similar couple Bm tries to bring the balance of force back into equilibrium. The degree of balancing force is, therefore, controlled by the area of the tailplane and the length of the tail moment arm. Hence aeroplanes with large tailplanes and/or long tail moments are very stable longitudinally. Good examples are the Sopwith $1\frac{1}{2}$ Strutter (large tailplane area), Avro 504 (long moment) both illustrated in the last chapter, and the BE 2c (enormous tailplane and good moment). This does not mean to say that models with fairly short moments and small tailplanes cannot be made to fly satisfactorily; both my Leopard Moth, which had a tailplane area of only 8 per cent of the wing area and the Hannover were very good fliers, but required careful trimming to avert any stalling tendency.

Of course, you can always cheat and increase the area of the tailplane in relation to the wings – a practice very popular in the old rubber-powered days – but generally this is unnecessary except in extreme cases which are best avoided anyway. No serious scale modeller today should consider increasing the tail area as he would be severely penalised in a competition.

One final word on tailplanes. I have found the symmetrical section, as opposed to the lifting section (Clark Y thinned), to be superior in all ways for scale models. Not only is it usually the section used on the full-sized prototype, but its symmetrical damping effect is more suited to scale models. I always set the tailplane parallel to the fuselage datum and attach the elevators with stiff alloy hinges. Trimming adjustments then can be made by setting the elevators to the desired angle. We shall deal with the construction of tailplanes later on.

(c) Directional stability

Generally, considerations of directional stability have little influence in the selection of a prototype. Most aeroplanes which are suitable in meeting the requirements of (a) and (b) will be directionally stable. Directional stability is the stability of an aircraft when turning about an axis vertically through the CG parallel to the fin. It is dependent on the position of the centre of lateral area (CLA). Referring to Fig. 2.3 it can be seen that the CLA, i.e. the centre of the total projected side areas, is well aft of the centre of gravity. This is common with most fairly short-nosed biplanes and a desirable feature. The 'weathercock' stability keeps the aircraft in a straight path, damping down any violent tendencies to turn. When the nose is longer, as in later inline-engined aeroplanes, then a larger fin is desirable to keep the CLA aft.

The effect of the gyrocouple and torque

Two further forces act on a propeller-driven aeroplane when under power. These are the gyrocouple and torque. The latter is generally fairly well understood and feared, the former, which on a free-flight scale model is far more important, less so. When viewed from the front, virtually all model

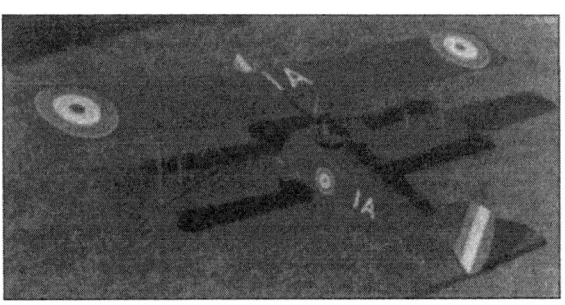

The RE 8 is a very stable aircraft due to the high CL, caused by having the top wing of greater area than the lower. This example was built by Terry Manley and won the Super Scale trophy in 1969.

aircraft engines rotate in an anti-clockwise direction, as do virtually all rubber model propellers. There is no reason for this, as far as I can see it is just convention, apart from the fact it is probably easier for a right-handed individual to flick in an anti-clockwise direction. Rotation is resisted by air drag on the propeller, creating a force tending to roll the whole aircraft in the opposite direction to that in which the propeller is turning. This torque reaction turns a normal model to the left.

The gyrocouple is rather more difficult to explain and I certainly do not intend to go into the mathematics of gyroscopes here. However, if you mount an engine on a hand-held board about 12in. square and run it, you will observe that if you turn the board sharply to the right, then the right-hand side of the board tries to dip. With a powerful engine you will find this dipping force is very strong, almost impossible to resist. Similarly, if you turn the board to the left, the left-hand side of the board lifts. It can therefore be seen that when fitted to a model these forces have an opposite effect to the torque. In a power model the gyroscopic forces are much greater than the torque. In a rubber model, with its slow-revving huge propeller, the torque effect is the greater.

The practical method of overcoming these forces on the free-flight power model is to apply right sidethrust to the engine and turn the aeroplane to the left under power. The amount of sidethrust can only usually be determined by practical trimming. In general the average biplane with medium power likes about 2 or 3 degrees. More powerful and fast-flying aircraft require more sidethrust. By turning to the left the inside wing is always being dragged up by the gyrocouple. Turns to the right under power usually end in disaster as the gyrocouple digs the inside wing further and further down so that eventually the model spirals into the ground. Models with a high degree of lateral stability, such as the Jüngmann, will turn in wide circles to the right but the risk of a spiral is always there.

Well, that concludes our brief look at the problem of stability and the ways in which we try to make the natural forces keep our model flying on an even keel. So far I have not mentioned the use of pendulums as an aid to natural stability. I must be quite frank here and say I do not think much of them. I have experimented with them on two models many years ago and found them more trouble than they are worth. Nevertheless several prominent scale modellers have appeared to use them with success in the past, notably the late P. E. Norman and more recently John Simmance. My own thoughts, for what they are worth, are that 90% of scale models fitted with pendulums fly despite them, rather than assisted by them. Pendulums can be applied to operate ailerons, rudders or elevators. The linkage to operate the latter two controls being simpler than that to ailerons has resulted in their greater popularity although, if the system worked as intended, aileron control should be the best. The idea of pendulum control is that irrespective of the attitude the aeroplane gets itself into, the pendulum will always hang vertically, linkage between the pendulum being arranged to apply corrective forces to the appropriate flying control to bring the aeroplane back to an even keel again.

All this works perfectly – when the aeroplane is held stationary and rotated about its various axes. Unfortunately, when flying, the pendulum is also subjected to various inertia forces, apart from gravity, which upsets the idea somewhat. The first of these is apparent when you try to hand-launch the model. The pendulum moves aft and applies down elevator. Not the ideal control force for a smooth getaway!

Some years ago I discussed the inertia problem with John Simmance. He considered he had overcome the difficulty by limiting the amount of control movement to only a few degrees so that it couldn't get the model into any real trouble. If this was the case, however, neither would it get it out of any stability trouble. I am convinced his models possessed sufficient inherent stability, not only to overcome natural unstabilising forces, but those also applied by the pendulum! I am sure John and a lot more scale modellers would disagree with me. What has been proved, however, is that there are great numbers of aeroplanes that can be made to fly well without any artificial stability means, so why increase a model's complexity and weight?

Some suggested prototypes

Many people ask what is a suitable choice for a beginner to scale modelling, or would such and such make a good model. Perhaps the following 'recommended' listing, roughly categorised, may assist you in your choice.
(1) Very stable, sturdy and not overblessed with detail, making them ideal beginners' subjects.
  (a) *WWI subjects*
     Bristol Scout D, S2A, M1 monoplane
     Martinsyde S2, Elephant
     Sopwith Tabloid, Baby, $1\frac{1}{2}$ Strutter
  (b) *Between wars*
     Avro Baby, Avian
     De Havilland 60 Moth, 82a Tiger Moth, 87b Hornet Moth
     Mitsubishi IMFI

BU 133b Jüngmann, Stampe SV4B
Blackburn Bluebird
(2) Fairly stable subjects but offering greater structural difficulties and/or much greater detail, such as exposed engines.
   (a) *WWI subjects*
      Armstrong Whitworth FK 3, FK 8
      Avro, 504 series
      BE 2C, D and E, BE 12a and b
      Blackburn 1912 Monoplane, White Falcon
      De Havilland 4, 6, 9 and 9a
      Martinsyde Buzzard
      RE 8
      SE 5
      Sopwith Pup and Triplane
      Hannover CL IIIa
      Rumpler C series
      Albatros CIII
      Breguet 14
      Nieuport 28
   (b) *Between wars*
      Armstrong Whitworth Siskin IIIa
      Avro Tutor
      Blackburn B2, Dart, Ripon
      Gloster Gauntlet, Gladiator
      Fairey Gordon, IIIF, Flycatcher

The De Havilland Leopard Moth, always a popular subject with excellent inherent stability. Its 'brother' design, the Puss Moth, is perhaps slightly more popular by virtue of its larger wing area.

SELECTION OF PROTOTYPE

A diminutive DH Hornet Moth flown by L. Perring at Old Warden, using a Cox ·010 motor. Proves that small glow motors can be used in suitable in-line prototypes provided the prop can 'see' some air.

Hawker Hart series, Nimrod, Woodcock, Tomtit
Vickers Vildebeest
Westland Wapiti, Lysander
Heinkel 51
Focke Wulf 44 Stieglitz

The foregoing are just a selection and are not intended to be a complete listing in any way – they are predominantly British, and have a touch of personal preference amongst them! Certainly, if built carefully, none should prove difficult to trim. You will note that the most glamorous fighters of World War I are omitted i.e. the Camel, Fokker D7, Albatros DV and Spad S7. I am not saying that a skilled person cannot make them fly, but they are certainly tricky, all lacking natural stability – which, of course, is why they were such good mounts. No account has been taken as to the ease in which constructional details can be obtained – some are very well documented, whereas others offer a much greater challenge.

CHAPTER 3

Design Features

In Chapter 2 we considered the aerodynamic and stability aspects which govern the selection of a suitable prototype. We will now look at a few mechanical aspects, particularly with regard to biplanes, which may also influence our choice.

At this stage I think it may be an opportune time to refer to nomenclature used for the various parts of a biplane. Although these terms may be familiar to some, I find more and more younger people are confused by some of the names of the various struts and wires. As we shall refer to these parts quite a lot both in this and future chapters, a study of Fig. 3.1 should be worthwhile if you do not quite know the difference between a cabane and an interplane strut.

Biplanes normally fall into two classes: single bay and double bay. Most small biplanes, including the majority of single seat fighters, fall into the single bay category while most two seaters are usually rigged as double bayed machines. Occasionally you come upon a three bayed machine but these are

The Westland Lysander is an aircraft which many have tried to model, though seldom with success in respect of flying performance due to high wing loadings caused by the enormous fuselage.

―――――― DESIGN FEATURES ――――――

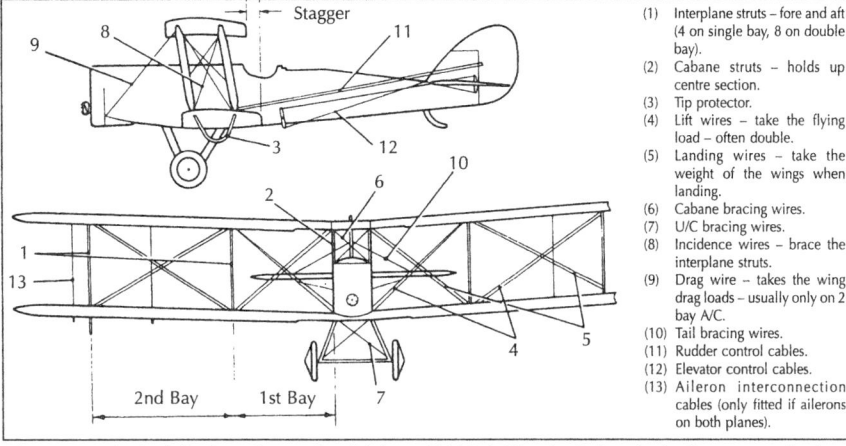

(1) Interplane struts – fore and aft (4 on single bay, 8 on double bay).
(2) Cabane struts – holds up centre section.
(3) Tip protector.
(4) Lift wires – take the flying load – often double.
(5) Landing wires – take the weight of the wings when landing.
(6) Cabane bracing wires.
(7) U/C bracing wires.
(8) Incidence wires – brace the interplane struts.
(9) Drag wire – takes the wing drag loads – usually only on 2 bay A/C.
(10) Tail bracing wires.
(11) Rudder control cables.
(12) Elevator control cables.
(13) Aileron interconnection cables (only fitted if ailerons on both planes).

Figure 3.1. *Typical rigging of a two bay biplane (DH 9a). The single bay is similar except the inner bay is omitted.*

usually multi-engined machines which are best left alone. Most biplanes are rigged positive, or forward, stagger; quite a number have no stagger at all and

The Gloster Gladiator possesses ideal configuration for free flight and is a most attractive craft. The upper picture shows the Shuttleworth Collection's version, while below is an example destined for the RAF Museum.

―――――――――――27―――――――――――

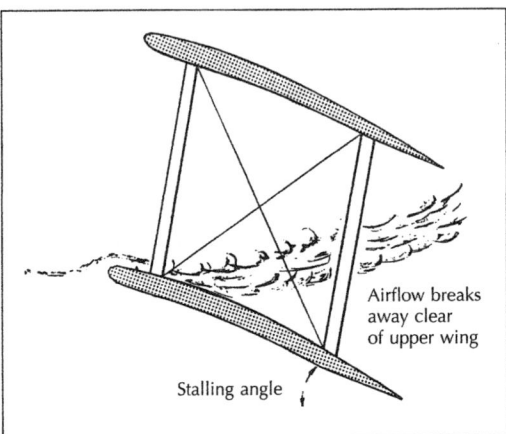

Figure 3.2. *Forward staggered wings stalled (minimal interference).*

just a few have negative, or back stagger. The DH 5 and Beech 17 are possibly the best known examples, although back stagger machines are best avoided owing to their inherent poor stall recovery problems. The main reason for forward stagger is to reduce the airflow interference between the two planes; if this stagger is reversed the upper wing is in the backwash of the lower wing when stalled. Automatic stall recovery is very slow with this layout and most builders of back stagger models have found the ground has hit the model before it has managed to recover! See Figs 3.2 and 3.3.

A lot of modellers avoid two bay biplanes because of the extra set of interplane struts and doubling up of wires which is a pity, because some of the best flying scale subjects are amongst this category. Virtually all the stable two seaters of the 1914–18 war were thus rigged, very little extra work is required in two bay rigging and there are some advantages.

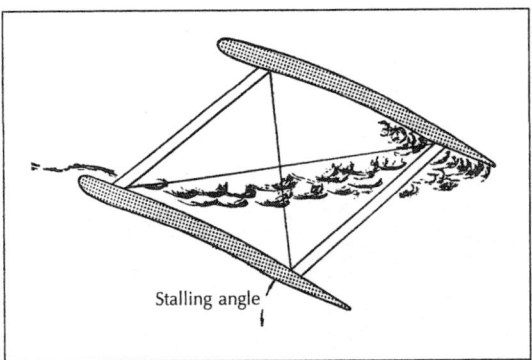

Figure 3.3. *Back staggered wings stalled. The upper wing is completely in the backwash of the lower wing causing violent stalling characteristics and poor recovery properties.*

———————————— DESIGN FEATURES ————————————

Figure 3.4. Section used on Hawker biplanes.

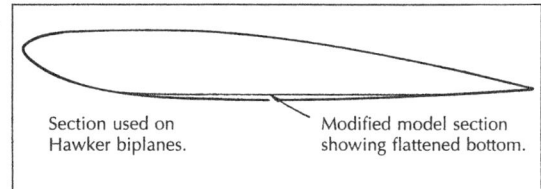

Section used on Hawker biplanes.   Modified model section showing flattened bottom.

We must now consider wing sections. Most aeroplanes of the 1914–18 period used RAF 15 or very similar undercambered sections. This is an excellent model flying section, its only drawback being that it is somewhat on the thin side. However, if we are to reproduce the character of the original, both in appearance and flying performance, it is essential that we do not deviate very much from the original. Some degree of thickening, 20% at the most, is permissible if structural considerations demand it. This is not really necessary however, provided that some degree of the flying load is carried by the rigging. I have no time for the people who thicken up the wings to a Clark Y type of section and then produce a pair of cantilever wings; using the rigging, if they fit it, purely for ornament. Such methods should be reserved strictly for Fokkers! With later types of aeroplane when a bi-convex section was used then some modification can be introduced to the benefit of the flying performance, without noticeably detracting from the appearance of the model. Fig. 3.4 shows the flattening of the undersurface of the bi-convex section I used on the Nimrod; the flat bottom makes for easier building and also slows the flying speed down, always a desirable feature, as most model aircraft fly in excess of scale speed.

I have mentioned that invariably thin symmetrical sections are used in full-size practice, at least up to 1940 anyway, for tail surfaces. These should be adhered to implicitly as nothing looks worse than thick tail surfaces.

Kit manufacturer Veron recognised the potential of the Hawker Tomtit, although its version is intended for R/C use only. The upper and lower wings are identical in construction, a good labour-saving point!

Ideal power units in my eyes are these 'old timers', the Mills .75cc (top left) with the ED Bee Mk. 1 next to it. Below left is the ED Racer and finally the Mills 1.3cc. Few modern engines are really suitable for scale work though increasing numbers of long-stroke replicas are being made, including reduced size versions of larger originals.

We will now look at suitable engines for free-flight scale models. These are somewhat different from other classes of model, the main requirements being:
(1) Ability to swing a large diameter propeller in relation to its capacity.
(2) Ease of cowling.
(3) Ease of starting and ability to run with poor cooling without protesting.
(4) Controllability.
In order to achieve (1) a fairly long stroke is necessary. Because of cowling difficulties the rotary shaft valve engine is most unsuitable. Rear induction is most desirable, either by rotary disc valve, or sideport in the cylinder. Without doubt, the old-fashioned long stroke engine with sideport induction is by far the most suitable. The throttle and choke can be approached by removal of the upper rear part of the cowling, usually following a scale break line. The fuel line is easier to route also. Perhaps the only drawback of this type of

DESIGN FEATURES

engine is its height which may be difficult to accommodate in the cowling of a small model. Invariably these engines start easily and because they do not rev very fast, run fairly cool and do not worry very much about being almost totally cowled, although some degree of airflow through the cowling is essential. Several engines of this type are once again being manufactured today and are vastly superior for our purposes than the small glow motors offered in profusion by the model trade which are totally unsuitable for our use. They will not turn a propeller large enough to clear the cowling of the average scale model, nor is controllability one of their strong virtues. Some of the larger glow motors, developed for radio control use, are much better in both respects but are generally too large for our use. Some of the modern small diesels manufactured in the UK can be used quite successfully but being chiefly rotary shaft valve types suffer installation problems accordingly. They will, however, turn reasonable sized propellers.

In my view two engines stand out above all others as free-flight scale power units – the Mills 0.75cc and its bigger brother the Mills 1.3cc. These two engines will power virtually all models the free-flight modeller should wish to build. The 0.75cc is happy with models down to 25in. span ranging up to about 36in. in the case of a biplane, and 40in. as a monoplane. If the model is very light and has low drag these sizes can be exceeded but I do not recommend this practice as you have no reserve of power, if the model turns out overweight (they usually do), or for flying in a breeze. Remember you can always reduce the power on too powerful a motor, but you cannot make it

Both the Avro 504 (in the foreground) and the DH Tiger Moth are each in their own right very popular subjects – both these examples being preserved for the RAF Museum. The 'Tigger', a superb flying performer, is an all-time favourite.

produce more than it is capable of. The 1.3cc takes over where the 0.75cc leaves off and will power a biplane up to 50in. span and about 36oz in weight, and monoplanes up to 60in. span.

You have to be very careful however about power units, particularly with biplanes, when the span exceeds 40in. A model of a single seat fighter will require considerably greater power than a two seater of similar span, a good example being the RE 8 of Terry Manley illustrated previously which spanned 52in. and flies well on a Mills 1.3cc. Compare this with my SE 5a also illustrated earlier which only spanned $45\frac{1}{2}$ in. and yet required an ETA 15 flat out to fly it properly. The answer, of course, lies in the relative drag and weight of the two aeroplanes. The cross sectional area of the fuselage of the SE 5a is much greater than the RE 8, also, although smaller in span, the wings have considerably greater chord. I would not recommend that single seater fighter biplanes are built to such a large scale as my SE 5a (1/7) as invariably they are rather heavy and require a lot of power, making them difficult to trim and rather unforgiving in a prang.

While we are digressing about sizes, let me say that I think that for general fun flying the ideal size for a free-flight scale model is about 30in.–36in. and

Three privately owned DH Hornet Moth biplanes display a variety of colour schemes. An ideal first subject to choose due to the simplicity of the cowling engine, lack of centre section struts and good general proportions. Rather surprisingly, modellers seemed to have overlooked this sleek design.

The top three photographs depict DH Puss Moths, while the lower one is a Leopard Moth – the undercarriage and wing plan being the distinguishing feature. These monoplanes share a similar fuselage with the Hornet Moth (see opposite). Even in monoplane form, this aircraft has seldom been tackled, despite the relative ease with which they may be viewed for additional detail information.

the weight, even on a well-detailed model, should not exceed 20oz. I find this class of model by far the easiest to trim and fly; if you make a mistake trimming, more often than not it 'bounces' without more than superficial damage. The larger model is more suited to competition flying as it enables a greater amount of detail to be incorporated. However, the weight climbs rapidly with increase in span and 'bouncability' is rapidly replace by 'crunchability'.

Returning to power units, apart from the Mills pair, other suitable units made in the past and sometimes available on the second-hand market are the Amco 0.87cc, very rare these days, and the ED Mk. 1cc Bee, the latter usefully providing a squat power unit between the two Mills engines in power

An unusual engine for free-flight scale use is the ETA 15 diesel, seen here mounted on a 10 gauge light alloy plate in the nose of my SE 5a. Few scale models use engines of such power and capacity, but the large wing area of this subject required an engine capable of turning a large propeller. Judging by the 'shaved' cylinder fins, this motor has seen life in an FA1 team racer!

output. For people who like to build big and require something with more power than the 1.3 then, without doubt, the best unit is the old ED 2.4cc Racer, now making a welcome return back into production. Although relatively short stroked, this engine will turn a useful sized propeller and is a good starter as well as being very controllable. I cannot recommend the old ED 2cc engines, although they are reasonably plentiful on the second-hand market; they vibrate rather a lot and are just that bit too tall for cowling on all but the bulkiest models. Neither can I recommend the big Mills 2.4cc which had a relatively short production run. Although, like its small brethren, it was beautifully made it is rather a bad-mannered engine, being very fussy about carburation as well as being very tall.

You will have noticed that all the engines I recommend are diesels. Apart from its ability to swing a large prop, the diesel is also more suitable because it does not require the chore of attaching a starting battery, and the fuel it uses will not attack cellulose finishes, which I find superior to all others for scale work. I always use fuel of my own mix using mineral oil (Castrol GTX) in preference to castor. This can be wiped off from the airframe much more easily than the gooey mess that castor oil leaves, so preserving the appearance of the machine for a much longer period. Although castor oil is a superior lubricant for hot running, high revving engines, mineral oil is quite adequate for the type of engine used for scale models.

―――――――― CHAPTER 4 ――――――――

Fuselage Construction

It is now time that we get down to examining the structure of the free-flight scale model. In general this is very similar to any other type of free-flight model, except that often parts which are stressed to a higher degree than is normal call for the substitution of hardwoods, or metal, where balsa would be normal practice. With a scale model you are stuck with the shape provided, unlike on a functional flying model where very often the design is a compromise between aerodynamics, strength and lightness. As balsa possesses a very high strength to weight ratio the shape can be adjusted accordingly so that it can be utilised to the maximum. Unfortunately, with scale models very often balsa just is not strong enough, within the confines allowed, and stronger and, regrettably, heavier woods have to be resorted to. The structure of a scale model should not only be strong, but, just as important, flexible. A structure that deflects when it hits the ground awkwardly will be much lighter than one strong enough to stand the blow rigidly – by making a flexible structure we can crack the weight/strength vicious circle. The best materials from which to base a flexible structure are

Uncovered view of a Hawker Nimrod reveals the sturdy structure. Light construction of a scale model is essential – the old axiom of 'the bigger they come, the harder they fall' is most true. A good example of a typical scale fuselage – sheeted frontal portion with fabric-covered, multi-stringered rear.

Looking every inch the classic biplane, my $\frac{1}{12}$ th scale Sopwith $1\frac{1}{2}$ Strutter is very hard to distinguish from the full size in this low-angle shot – only the airscrew and prop nut identify it as a model. Note how provision of a pilot completes the realism.

Completed Hawker Nimrod clearly displays the multi-stringed rear fuselage. This model uses a 'flattened' bi-convex section, as described in Chapter 3, which makes building easier while slowing down the flying speed.

FUSELAGE CONSTRUCTION

spruce and piano wire, both of which are used in considerable quantities in our models. Balsa, however, remains the most common material and must be used wherever possible to keep the weight to a minimum. Plywood also features largely in the structure of a scale model – this must be of the highest aircraft quality, 2mm for bulkheads and 0.8mm for decking being the most useful thicknesses.

Modern adhesives form a very important part in construction today and have really made possible great advances in the scale modeller's art. Over forty years ago, when cellulose balsa cement was the only adhesive available, the joining of wood to metal was a nightmare of binding with cotton of every single fitting. Epoxy resin adhesives have mercifully changed all that although, for very highly stressed wire to wood joints, some binding assistance still doesn't come amiss. PVA white glue is a far better adhesive for spruce than balsa cement, as indeed it is for the majority of balsa joints, especially when sheeting. The fact that it does not shrink when drying prevents warping of delicate structures fabricated from 1/32in. sheet.

Let us now consider the fuselage structure in detail. Fuselages can be simple box or round sections covered in fabric, plywood or metal – they are usually a combination of some, or all, of these materials. A good example is the Hawker Nimrod which features a basic box on which formers and stringers are superimposed at the aft end and metal panels (on the original) used at the nose end. In general we should try to stick to the original form of construction as closely as possible. Therefore, if the original was fabric covered we should represent all ribs, stringers and structure that shows through and cover with tissue and silk (we shall deal with covering fully later on). If the original structure was covered with ply then we should use either thin ply, or better still, sheet balsa, if suitable. Generally ply is more suitable for the decking of fuselages, particularly if there are a lot of cutouts, as sheet balsa tends to split under such circumstances. Although heavier, a lot of this weight can be recovered, as only a very sparse supporting structure is required. Similarly, if the original had metal stressed skin covering then balsa sheet, or ply, should be used. If the prototype was painted then no further treatment is required, but, if the metal was left natural then some form of metallising of the wood covering will be necessary – this too will be covered in a later chapter on finishing.

Selection of material for the longerons depends upon the size and construction of the fuselage. On aeroplanes between about 30in. and 50in. span, $\frac{1}{8}$in. sq is the most common size for box-type fuselages. Hard balsa is good enough for the smaller models, but spruce is the most universally used material. On large models, $\frac{3}{16}$ in. sq is sometimes used, if strength demands it, but it generally looks too heavy through the covering. If the fuselage is multi-stringered, to give a rounded form as on the Nimrod, then balsa longerons should be used to save weight, but the stringers, $\frac{1}{16}$ in. sq or $\frac{3}{32}$ in. sq, dependent on the size, should be spruce. Balsa stringers are too brittle for the amount of handling a scale fuselage gets, also they tend to pull in over the years due to the tension of the covering, giving the rather unattractive 'starved horse' appearance.

Formers should be varied according to the loading they will receive. You should not be afraid to make really beefy structures at the nose end as weight saving is a waste of time forward of the CG. Ballast very often has to be added in any case on the average short-nosed model. Conversely, the structure should be as light as possible aft of the CG as, remember, one quarter of an ounce saved at the tail end can prevent up to 2 ounces of ballast being added in the nose. Good solid ply formers 2mm (or even 3mm in larger models) thick should be used to carry the engine bearers and undercarriage. The bearers should be of good section, $\frac{1}{2}$ in. × $\frac{3}{8}$ in. for a 1.3cc, and if possible glued to the sides of the fuselage – it is usually sheeted with $\frac{1}{8}$ in. balsa, between the longerons, in this region. If the fuselage is wide enough, and it usually is, the engine is not mounted directly on the bearers but attached via a 10 swg light alloy engine plate, which not only promotes a very strong structure but also allows the thrust line to be altered fairly easily if found necessary, as so often is the case, when trimming. If the sidethrust has to be altered more than a degree or so then usually a new engine plate is necessary. This, however, is infinitely better than slotting the holes in the bearers which would be the case if the engine was mounted direct. Slotted holes not only weaken the bearers but the engine very often alters its thrust line in a heavy landing – which then results in an even heavier landing on the next flight! A new engine plate also allows the crankcase to be displaced sideways, if the sidethrust is to be altered, so keeping the crankshaft emerging through the same hole in the front of the fuselage and not through the first exhaust stack!

All the basic structures at the front of the fuselage i.e. the ply formers, bearers and fuselage sides, should be glued together with an epoxy resin. I have found no other type of glue to be strong enough to withstand the constant battering from heavy landings and the effects of diesel fuel over the years.

Formers, aft of the wings, should be very light – $\frac{3}{32}$ in. or $\frac{1}{16}$ in. being quite strong enough – if any are required at all. Similarly cross members, which should be spruce at the front, should be medium balsa aft of the wing.

FUSELAGE CONSTRUCTION

Undercarriages

This is one of the most important items on a scale model and often requires the greatest working out. The problem is that the full-sized aircraft's gear is designed to land on a smooth surface, at stalling speed, in which the vertical component is of far greater importance than the horizontal, or drag, component. The undercarriage is therefore designed to have a considerable vertical travel and very little, if any, horizontal travel.

Unfortunately, a free-flight model is not able to choose a nice smooth place to land nor is it able to stall, or flare as it is generally known, at the correct moment. It therefore lands at a speed considerably in excess of scale; particularly if it is pointed downwind at the time as is usually the way of things. Our horizontal, or drag, component is usually very much greater than our vertical component. We therefore require our undercarriage to have a large amount of horizontal travel with very little vertical travel – converse to the design of the scale structure we wish to model.

On very light models you can ignore the problem and produce a rigid structure, with no backward travel, as I did on my Sopwith $1\frac{1}{2}$ Strutter built over thirty years ago. This model was built to 1/12 scale and weighed about

The collapsed undercarriage on Terry Manley's Armstrong Whitworth FK 8 illustrates how main legs do all the work while the remaining struts are virtually 'collapsible ornaments'.

—39—

16oz when new, which is probably about the limit for an unsprung (in the backward sense that is) undercarriage. The model lasted for some eight years of fairly intensive flying although occasionally the rear struts buckled and had to be re-straightened. The only springing the unit possessed was of the scale, vertical variety i.e. double fixed spreader bars keep the two undercarriage vees apart and a split axle is hinged in the centre. The springing is provided by rubber bands lashed round the ends of the axle and spreader bars, the only snag with these being that they rot with the fuel, which runs down the legs, and require regular replacements.

For models heavier and larger than the $1\frac{1}{2}$ then some form of backward springing is a must if we are not to be continually repairing the undercarriage. I have tried many forms of springing, on various models, but have yet to find anything which approaches the torsion bar in performance. Irrespective of how many struts and stays the undercarriage may have, it will always possess a pair of main legs which are usually more or less vertical and carry the wheels. These legs should form the working part of the torsion bar undercarriage – all the remaining struts etc. can be regarded as collapsible ornaments.

This view of the Hawker Nimrod's undercarriage clearly shows a working example of the unit drawn in Figure 4.1 and described in the text. Balsa fairings are epoxied to the 10 swg legs.

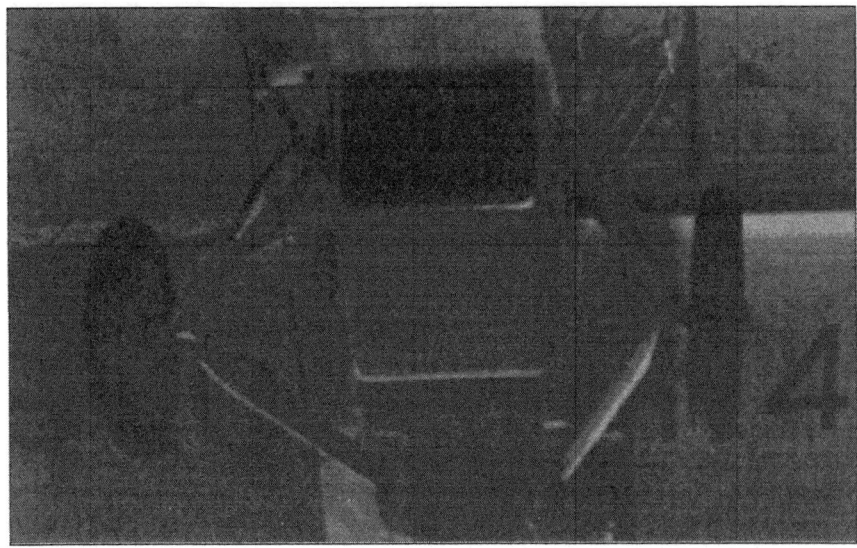

Figure 4.1. *It is not difficult to make J bolts to hold a torsion bar undercarriage but accurate bending of 10 or 12 swg piano wire takes a little practice.*

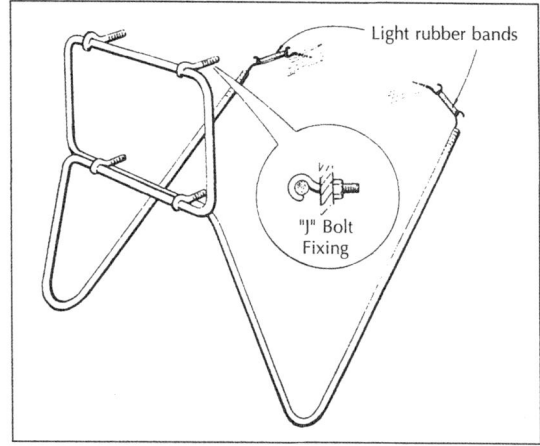

Fig. 4.1 shows a typical torsion bar undercarriage, as may be applied to a V undercarriaged machine. The undercarriage is bent from one piece of 12 swg piano wire (use 10 swg for larger models) and is then secured to a 2mm or 3mm ply former with J bolts. It is best to extend the engine bearers back to this former so that the torsion loads can be distributed more efficiently into the fuselage structure. J bolts can easily be made by cutting the head off a 1in. long 6BA screw, heating it up to red heat with a torch, while held in a vice, and bending the end to shape with pliers.

All landing loads are absorbed by the twisting of the wire in the double section at the bottom of the fuselage. An undercarriage of this type will take a slight 'set' the first time it is bent but, thereafter, will always return to the same set position. It is therefore advisable to bend the undercarriage with the legs having a slightly forward rake, so that when the set takes place, the legs are at their correct angle. The rear struts are continuations of the main legs, bent back to form a vee and made extra long so that they pass through slots in the bottom of the fuselage and serve no structural purpose, merely sliding through the slots when the main legs bend back. I have found that these rear legs tend to thresh about in a heavy landing if they have no location, so I always solder 20 swg hooks to their ends and keep them pulled against the front of the slots by means of light rubber bands stretching from these hooks to a suitable anchorage on a bulkhead. I must emphasise, however, that these bands are not a part of the springing system – the torsion bar absorbs all the landing loads. A 12 swg or 10 swg axle is attached to the apex of the vee, either sprung by rubber bands, as previously described, or bound with fuse

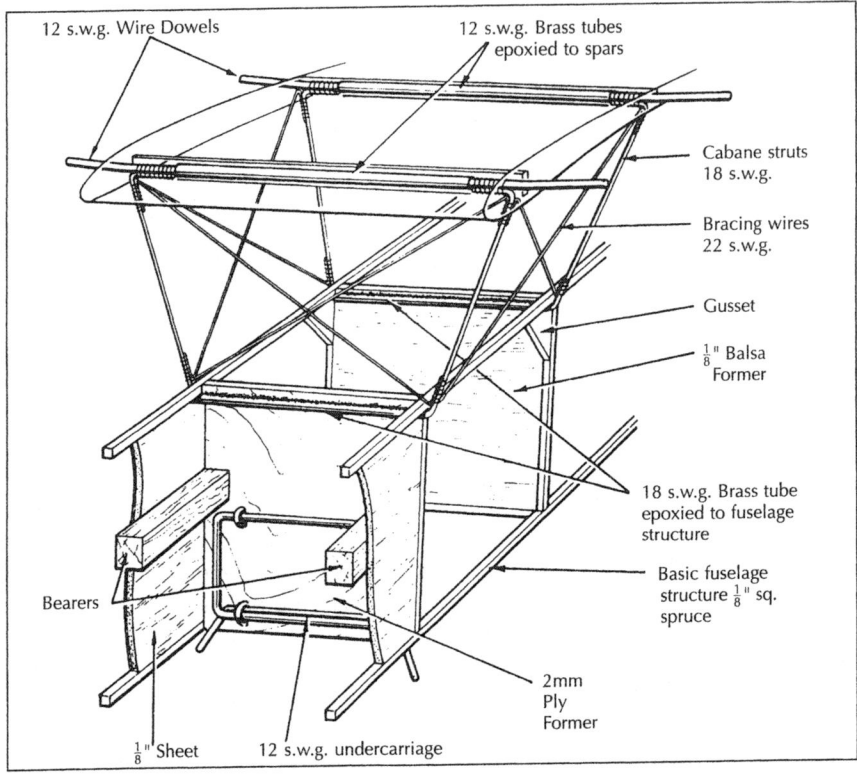

Figure 4.2. A typical biplane cabane shown with fairings omitted for clarity.

wire and soldered. Balsa fairings epoxied and bound, either with cotton or strips of tissue, complete the undercarriage.

Cabanes

The structure which holds the upper wings of most biplanes above the fuselage is known as the cabane. It usually is attached to a short section of wing known as the centre section, as on the Nimrod, or the main planes may be attached directly to it as in the case of the $1\frac{1}{2}$ Strutter. Sometimes in cabin biplanes, such as the DH Hornet Moth, both the upper wings are attached directly to the top of the fuselage.

Where applicable, a good strong, yet flexible, cabane structure is the heart of a successful model biplane. The only suitable material for its construction

FUSELAGE CONSTRUCTION

is piano wire, balsa fairings being added where necessary purely for appearance. The design of the cabane of the prototype we are modelling should be studied very carefully to see how the loads, carried by the centre section, are taken to the fuselage structure. On a model the cabane structure will be subjected to considerable twisting, sideways and inertia loads, imparted by the wings in an awkward landing. It is therefore imperative that every wire is made to work, just as on the original, if our centre section is not to collapse early in its lifetime. To make a four-strutted structure and omit the bracing wires, or use elastic thread, is just not good enough. Fig. 4.2 illustrates a typical cabane structure, showing how each bracing wire is anchored to do its particular job. Of course a bracing wire can only stabilise the structure in one direction (with the wire in tension) and another similar wire, usually the opposite diagonal, must take the reverse load. The scantlings, also indicated on Fig. 4.2, are suitable for a single seater of about 36in. span or a two seater around 46in. span (about 1/10 scale for

Holding my Nimrod and conferring with J. Archbold of Leicester holding his model of John Isaac's man-carrying model Fury at a rally for scale models held at Old Warden.

1914–18 jobs). For larger machines the wire sizes should go up a couple of gauges, i.e. the undercarriage and dowels should be 10 swg and the cabane struts made from 16 swg. It will be noted that the front of the cabane and the undercarriage coincide on the same former – this is very often the case. This former is the most heavily loaded on the entire model and, as mentioned earlier, if at all possible the bearers should run back into it. Everything in this region should be glued with epoxy.

The brass tube at the bottom of the cabane struts is threaded onto the wire prior to bending. The fore and aft cabane struts are then bent as individual pairs and great care should be taken in getting the lengths of the cabane struts exactly right as they control the incidence of the upper wing. The brass tubes are then epoxied to the fuselage structure and allowed to set for 24 hours before any further work is done on the cabane structure. At this stage the fore and aft struts should be able to revolve freely in their respective tubes, which is essential because it allows the completed cabane to 'work' without cracking the epoxied joints. The wing dowels are now bound to the top of the cabane struts with fuse wire and soldered.

Another view of the AW FK 8 illustrates a typical centre-sectionless model. Both the figures are carved from balsa – a painstaking job – but one which is well rewarded when properly executed. Nothing looks worse than an empty cockpit when the model flies past the judges!

FUSELAGE CONSTRUCTION

After experimenting with many types of wing fixing, I find the piano wire dowel superior to all others for biplanes. They should protrude about 1in. from the centre section and locate in brass tubes epoxied to the spars of the respective wings. I shall deal with fixing in detail later.

It is advisable to make the centre section structure at this time and this should be built along the lines of the main planes, the structure of which will be dealt with later. The centre section should be offered up to the wing dowels and the incidence checked, and then they may be epoxied together. It is advisable to omit any sheeting of the centre section structure at this stage. Finally, the bracing wires are accurately bent to shape, then bound and soldered to the cabane struts. The centre section can then be completed and the fairings epoxied to the cabane struts.

It is usually most convenient to construct the cabane onto the basic box fuselage before any top decking, cockpits etc. are fitted; even if this does make top sheeting more difficult after the bracing wires are in place. If a centre section is not fitted the cabane structure is much simplified. In this case, such as with the FK 8, the cabane struts are much heavier gauge wire (12 swg) bent over and crossed at their apex to form the wing attachment dowels. A single 14 swg wire holds the fore and aft struts apart – it goes without saying that a good soldered joint is essential at each apex.

All cabanes are variations of the above two themes and it cannot be stressed enough that a good job should be made of this part. If a wire is bent a bit too long, or short, throw it away and make another – if the cabane is not right the model is doomed to failure. It is one part of the model where weight cannot be saved. Piano wire is heavy but nothing approaches it for strength and flexibility, so it is useless to try to substitute lighter materials; they will not withstand the bashing a cabane structure receives.

———————— CHAPTER 5 ————————

Rigging and Wing Attachment

There are basically two types of wing structure in which we are interested; those that are braced and cantilever wings. Almost all biplane wings, with the exception of Fokkers, fall into the former category, while monoplanes can be either. The bracing for a monoplane usually takes the form of parallel or vee struts, running from around the middle of the undersurface of the wings to the lower fuselage longerons. Earlier, i.e. mainly pre-1914, monoplanes were braced by a multiplicity of wires running to a kingpost above the fuselage and the undercarriage beneath it.

The reason for the division is that the biplane and braced monoplane wing structure is generally lighter and more flexible than the cantilever wing, which has to have heavy spars in order to carry the bending loads (due to lift and landing) without external assistance. Mechanically it is much more efficient to take out the lift loads through a high-tensile wire than in shear through a spar, but aerodynamically it is hopeless in terms of drag at speeds much in excess of 250 mph. The drag is not much of a worry to us in the free-flight scale world, but it must be appreciated that it results in a much higher rate of sink, with the engine cut, than a corresponding monoplane of similar weight. Also more power will be required to pull the externally braced machine through the air.

As the connection of the wing to the fuselage does not have to carry any bending load (I am speaking of full-sized practice now) only a shear load has to be carried, and the connection is usually made by means of a fork-end and pin. The spars have only to be sufficiently strong to carry the lift loads to the various attachment points of the wires and attachment pins. Invariably aeroplanes that are wire braced have two spars to which the interplane struts, in the case of a biplane, and the flying and landing wires are attached. The loads are therefore taken out at four places, in the case of a single bay, and six places in the case of a double bay machine. If we are to build a wing using

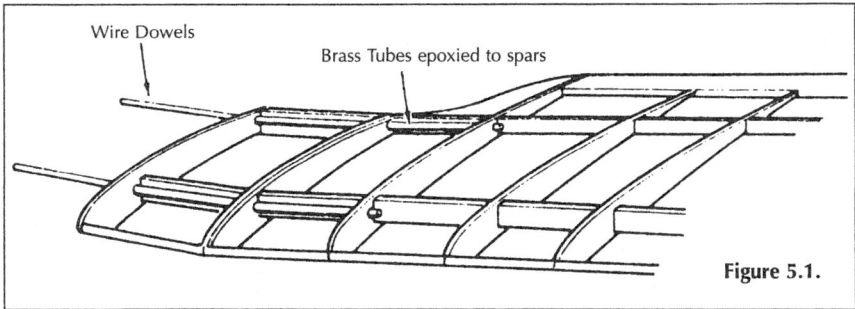

Figure 5.1.

something like the scale wing section the early machines used, it is essential that we take at least part of these loads out by these points.

Before looking at the wing structure in detail I intend to devote this entire chapter to the bracing, rigging and wing attachments for non-cantilevered models.

In Chapter 4 I stated that I considered the piano wire dowel to be the best form of wing attachment for biplanes that I know – it is also one of the simplest, and is shown in Fig. 5.1.

The wire dowels emerge from the centre section and engage with brass tubes passing through the first two ribs and epoxied to the forward face of the wing spars. This attachment will carry a considerable amount of bending, as well as shear, and if the dowels were substantial enough (10 swg for a 40in. span biplane) and provided the wings were thick enough for deep spars, as in the case of most biplanes of the 1930s, then no external bracing would be required. However, some method would have to be found to prevent the wing sliding off the dowels due to engine vibration, rigging normally performing this job. Provided the dowels are no longer than 1in., the wing will knock off, or at least 'give' sufficiently in a prang to reduce the risk of damage.

If the wing loads were taken entirely by the rigging wires then a pure shear connection of the wings to the centre section, and fuselage in the case of the lower wings, could be used. For many years I used stub birch dowels either $\frac{1}{8}$ in. or $\frac{3}{16}$ in. diameter, protruding approximately $\frac{1}{4}$ in., to effect such a wing fixing. The dowels located in the wing 'pick up' adjacent holes in the fuselage or centre section. Both end ribs need to be faced with 1mm ply to take the shear load and to avoid wearing out too rapidly. Although this method works well for the job intended and is very light, its drawback is that it tends to be too 'knockoffable'. With all but the smallest model anything heavier than a gentle landing results in the wings coming off and the subsequent collapse of

Top. The BE 12b uses the rigging system as shown in Figure 5.5 which provides an invisible method of attaching the wings, yet is still flexible enough to survive a prang. Bottom. Terry Manley's Armstrong Whitworth FK 8 uses shirring elastic most successfully as a rigging medium, although I prefer 'proper' bracing.

the wing cell, with wires and interplane struts flying everywhere. You then spend the next half hour playing that game, peculiar to the free-flight scale fraternity, known as 'hunt the landing wire'.

This problem can be overcome still using the stub dowel wing attachment, on two bay biplanes, by making the upper and lower wings of each side into a rigid cell. Either the rigging in the outer bays can be made solid with no give, achieved by rigidly attaching it to the respective spars, or the interplane strut attachments to the wing can be made stiff enough to carry bending loads. A simple method of doing this is to fret the interplane struts out of 2mm ply in pairs including a dummy section of rib as shown in Fig. 5.2.

Double ribs are fitted to the wing structure at the interplane strut stations. After the wing is covered the material is removed from between the ribs, and the necessary spars cut to allow the interplane struts to be inserted. Bracing wires in this case then can be of shirring elastic as it is called upon to do no work – the wing cell is quite stiff within itself. I used this method on my first powered free-flight scale model, the Avro 504 K, also on my DH 9a and finally on the Rumpler CV before abandoning the system. The major drawback of this system is that although it works extremely well when the wings receive a backwards blow, should the model fall on a wing tip then the bending load at the roots of the interplane struts very often fractures the plywood. The only possible repair is to remove the pair of interplane struts and fit new ones. After the third time you become bored with the operation! It is quite suitable though for a knockabout lightweight job. For a contest machine today, however, it is hopeless both from a strength point of view (contest winners are heavy) or from the appearance aspect. In my view, there are two other acceptable methods of attaching interplane struts to a wing,

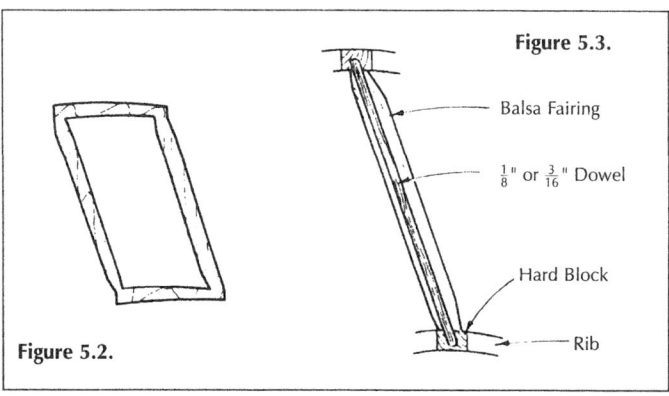

Figure 5.2.

Figure 5.3.
— Balsa Fairing
— $\frac{1}{8}$" or $\frac{3}{16}$" Dowel
— Hard Block
— Rib

both allowing the struts to be made individually. The first I used for many years, chiefly for single bay machines of which the Bucker Jüngmann and the Blackburn Ripon are examples.

Fig. 5.3 illustrates this type of strut which consists of nothing more than a $\frac{1}{8}$ in. dowel ($\frac{3}{16}$ in. for larger models) faired with hard balsa. The ends of the strut locate in hard balsa sockets glued to the spar and adjacent wing rib. Rubber bands are used for incidence wires and the tension of these keeps the strut pulled securely into its sockets. This is undoubtedly a very simple, light and neat interplane strut, very suitable for single bay machines, but unfortunately flies off rather easily in a prang, particularly if used with stub dowel wing attachments.

A type of fitting which holds the interplane struts more securely, yet is flexible in a heavy landing or crash, is shown in Fig. 5.4. Here the strut must be made of spruce, for strength, as it must take much more punishment than the fly-off variety.

The ends of the strut are slit with a junior hacksaw and a tinplate insert epoxied in. The 20 swg (18 swg for larger machines) clips are bent to be a tight fit on the spar to which they are epoxied after the wing cell has been temporarily rigged for the first time. The interplane struts can be retained either by a short piece of rubber tube (the insulation from 2 amp copper wire is ideal), or more permanently after the model is trimmed by soldered washers. This method of interplane strut retention is particularly suitable for N struts used on the last generation of biplanes such as the Nimrod, illustrated previously. For these later biplanes, which usually had small-section metal interplane struts, semi-flattened aluminium tubes are more suitable than spruce. The ends are hammered completely flat, filed to shape and drilled for the clips.

On the whole I think that this type of interplane strut system is the best developed to date. In a very bad crash it may smash a spar, but I have yet to

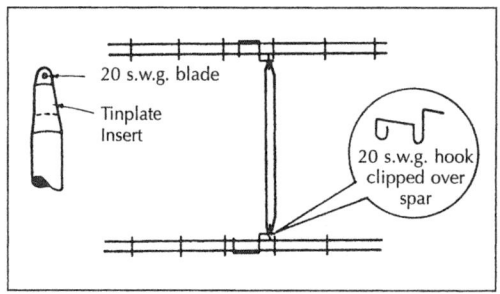

Figure 5.4. *My recommended wing strut fixing.*

RIGGING AND WING ATTACHMENT

Above. Another view of the FK 8 showing the piano wire hooks and eyes for fastening the shirring elastic. Struts are attached as per Figure 5.4. Below. My Bucker Jüngmann uses the 'plug-in' strut arrangement detailed in Figure 5.3.

suffer this although I have used it on my last three scale models. I have found it very suitable for two bay aeroplanes.

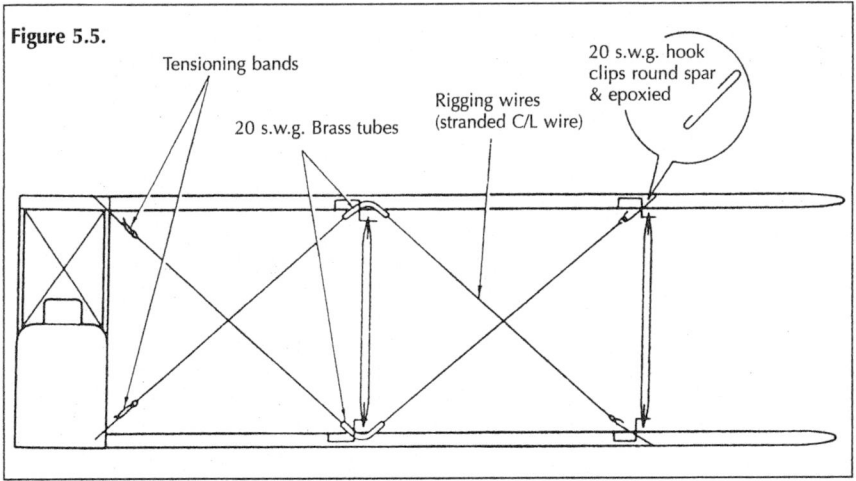

Figure 5.5.

We will now turn our attention to the main bracing wires, i.e. the flying and landing wires. If we wish these to do work then they must be either 24 swg or 22 swg piano wire, or even stranded control-line wire. If we only want our wires to be ornaments then shirring elastic, or golf ball elastic, is quite suitable. As I have stated before, I personally do not like to use elastic wires now – the last model I made using this technique was the Rumpler CV back in 1956. Several modellers, however, continue to use shirring elastic with great success – Terry Manley used such rigging on his AW FK 8. The shirring elastic rigging is usually retained with small S hooks made from soft 22 swg wire. Interplane struts are normally retained by the method illustrated in Fig. 5.4, but the wings must work as cantilevers when this form of rigging is used. However, when the wings are rigged in two bays, as the FK 8 is, a certain amount of girder effect takes place which prevents the wings from deflecting under load anything like as much as they would if completely independent. With a 1914–18 model, a certain amount of wing section thickening is almost inevitable to make the wing stiff enough.

The alternative to this method is to make the wires work as in the original. To me this has a satisfaction within itself – it makes more of a scale model.

Dealing with bracing the wing cell first, I would advocate the use of piano wire for single bay machines and stranded control-line wire for double bays. For single bay types, the wires are sprung by small rubber bands to 22 swg wire hooks to the wing spars, the rubber band substituting for the turnbuckle on the original. I used to employ rubber bands at each end of every wire, but

RIGGING AND WING ATTACHMENT

Centre section of my BE 12b typifies the wing attachment shown in Figure 5.1. It is extremely simple – the protruding wire dowels engaging in brass tubes within the wing panels – yet very strong, no external bracing being required.

nowadays find a single band, at the upper end as used on the Jüngmann, to be quite adequate.

You can use a similar technique for two bay machines but the number of wires tends to become excessive; at least 8 flying and 8 landing wires. If the wing cell collapses during a trimming session due to a hard landing, it would be dark before you had it rerigged ready for the next flight! I therefore advocate the method I have used with great success on my BE 12b, shown in Fig. 5.5. Only 4 wires per side are used, just as in a two bay machine, each wire acting as a landing wire in one bay and a flying wire in the next. The

The tail section of the same aeroplane illustrates an example of where I still prefer to use wire bracing rather than shirring elastic, mainly due to the latter's short life when in contact with diesel fuel.

A highly aerobatic two-seat trainer, the Bucker Jüngmann was long among my favourite subjects as I won several contests with models of this machine.

wires are led past the inner pair of interplane struts through 20 swg brass tubes, bent while hot to the shape required and epoxied to the appropriate wing spar. The wires are held in tension by rubber bands to small hooks attached to the centre section and fuselage. The tension in the wire produces sufficient friction between the wire and its guide tube to prevent the wing cell moving under normal flying and landing loads. However, if the model gets a heavy thump the whole lot distorts. When used in conjunction with wire dowels for wing retention, you have a beautifully flexible wing structure which is as near crash-proof as anything I have seen, as well as being very acceptable from a scale appearance point of view.

When wire is used for bracing parts of the structure other than the wings, it is not necessary, or indeed desirable, to spring the wire. Tail surfaces very often require bracing. If they are built to a scale thickness and light, as they

Figure 5.6. *Tailplane bracing.*

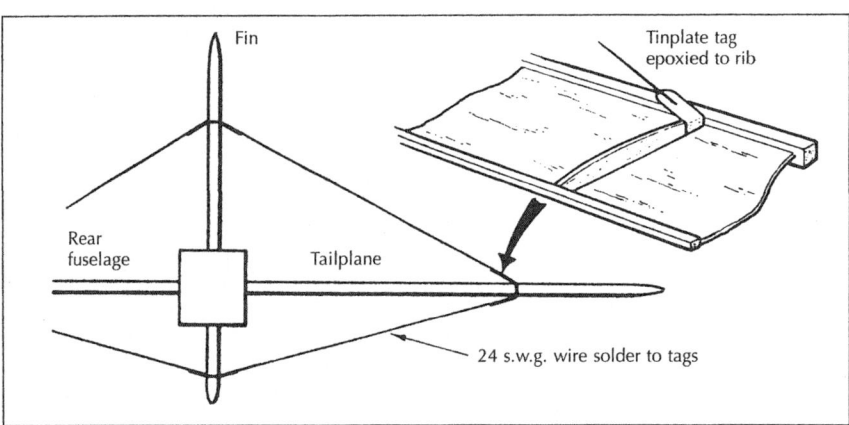

Ken McDonough's D-C Dart diesel-powered Instone Airlines DH 4a weighs only 8oz fully rigged and ready for free flight.

need to be, then solid bracing is very desirable to strengthen up the whole back end. It is usual with tail bracing of 1914–18 machines, when viewed from head on, that the total bracing forms a diamond, with the tail surfaces an enclosed cruciform. Without working steel bracing wires many of the large area tail surfaces of WWI types are very weak indeed; most tailplanes have a scale thickness of about $\frac{1}{8}$ in. or $\frac{3}{16}$ in., making them very whippy indeed. Of course, you *can* cheat and thicken the tailplane up, but this looks awful, so I therefore advocate the method illustrated in Fig. 5.6.

There is a strong case for using shirring elastic for the control wires although I often use 24 swg piano wire for this purpose. The one major objection I have to shirring elastic is that it rots in time due to fuel settling on it and requires replacement at intervals of about one year. It is much easier to use for control runs though, as it can be stretched to the required length.

It goes without saying that piano wire must be used for bracing those highly stressed units, the cabane and undercarriage.

I could go on *ad infinitum* on the subject of rigging wires. Everybody has their pet ideas and I know many people will not agree with mine. As will be gathered, I have altered my own ideas several times in the last twenty years and no doubt will do so again as new materials become available. I hope that within these pages something new and of interest to some has been put forward on this vexed subject.

CHAPTER 6

Wing and Tailplane Construction

We will look in detail at the structure of scale model tail surfaces prior to the wing structure. This is because I usually construct my wing tips in a similar manner to my tailplanes, and as this construction is somewhat unconventional I intend to devote a large part of this chapter to it.

Generally tail surfaces are the least well-made structure on the average scale model. Typical instructions given with most kits and magazine articles blandly state *the tailplane and fin should be constructed in a similar manner to the wings*, sometimes with a rider to the effect that *care should be taken to avoid warps*. I used to build my tail surfaces similar to my wings but stopped doing so after the Avro 504 K in 1951. Although I took care to avoid warps, it did not prevent me having to hold the thing in front of the electric fire every week and twist the tail surfaces flat again!

If a free-flight scale model is to have a long and successful life it is essential that the tail structure is built true and remains warp-free for its entire life. When you consider that the edges of the typical fabric-covered tailplane were usually metal tube of about 1in. to $1\frac{1}{2}$in. diameter this means that our edges must be made from $\frac{3}{32}$in. to $\frac{1}{8}$in. sq balsa (anything else would be too heavy) if working to approximately 1/12th scale. As the maximum tailplane thickness

Figure 6.1. *Cross section through tailplane.*

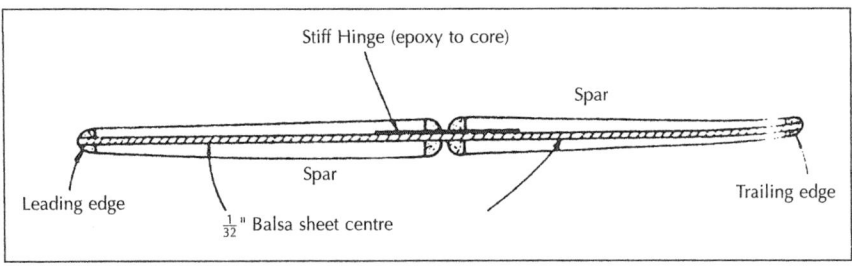

WING AND TAILPLANE CONSTRUCTION

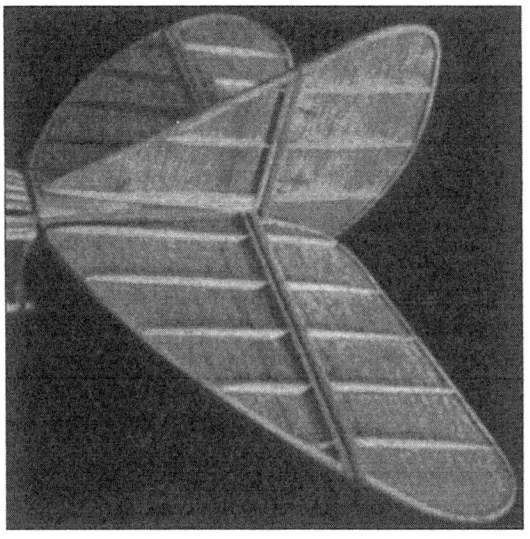

Detail shot of the Rumpler tail surfaces shows Figure 6.1 put into practice. The unit is very light, strong, warp-resistant yet looks 'right'. Note also the grain direction used in the fin/rudder – essential for greatest stiffness.

is about $\frac{3}{16}$ in., and the span can be up to 15in., an open framework similar to a wing structure cannot help but warp. If we stick to the open-framework structure the only alternative is to beef up the thickness and use oversized spars and edges. The result is most un-scale like in appearance.

Take a look at the photograph of the tail structure of my Rumpler CV built back in 1956. This is a sandwich form of construction which is built symmetrically over a centre core of $\frac{1}{32}$ in. sheet. Each part, i.e. tailplane, elevators, fin and rudder, is built separately as follows:

(1) Select a suitable piece of straight-grained medium hard $\frac{1}{32}$ in. sheet and place under the plan with a piece of carbon paper interposed.

(2) Draw over all the spar positions, leading and trailing edges and rib positions to transfer them, via the carbon paper, to the $\frac{1}{32}$ in. sheet.

(3) Cut out the sheet to outline shape.

(4) Draw a mirror image of the structure on the reverse side of the sheet. This is easily done by poking a pin through the sheet at each rib position where it joins the leading and trailing edges, and then joining all the holes up.

(5) Glue the structure to one side of the sheet preferably using a PVA adhesive to prevent warping. Pins are used to hold the strips in place until dry. The scantlings will depend on the model but for the Rumpler, which is a fairly typical 1914–18, 1/12th scale two seater spanning 45in. the

Uncovered view of my Rumpler CV displays the use of twin balsa spars let into the upper and lower surfaces of the rib. Although light and strong, my preference is now to use a centrally disposed spar as shown in Figure 6.2.

main spars were $\frac{1}{8}$ in. sq, the leading edges $\frac{3}{32}$ in. sq and the trailing edges $\frac{1}{16}$ in. sq. The ribs were $\frac{1}{16}$ in. × $\frac{1}{8}$ in. The spars should be medium hard but all the rest of the structure fairly soft. If the edges are curved, as on the Rumpler, then the balsa strip should be notched on the inside, with the thumbnail, at about $\frac{1}{8}$ in. to $\frac{1}{16}$ in. pitch, dependent on the radius, to pre-curve it prior to gluing to the sheet. You will be surprised how easily this is achieved. Practise first on a piece of scrap strip, holding it between the forefinger and thumbnail, then press. As you feed the strip through it forms a natural curve. The more notches per inch, the tighter the radius.

(6) When the structure is dry the sheet is turned over and the procedure repeated.

(7) Any 'hard points' to hold bracing wires or where the tailplane is attached to the fuselage etc., are now added.

(8) Using a glasspaper block, the whole structure is now sanded to the required airfoil shape, just like a chuck glider wing, although with considerably less effort and dust! A considerable amount of wood can be removed from the leading and trailing edges to get them nice and thin, as on the prototype. Care should be taken, however, not to overdo the sanding of ribs otherwise an unsightly scalloped effect is produced.

WING AND TAILPLANE CONSTRUCTION

Tail surfaces of the Hawker Nimrod illustrate the realistic appearance which can be obtained using the method described, and as illustrated in Figure 6.1. The sheet centre core cannot be seen, yet it prevents the tail from being 'transparent' in flight.

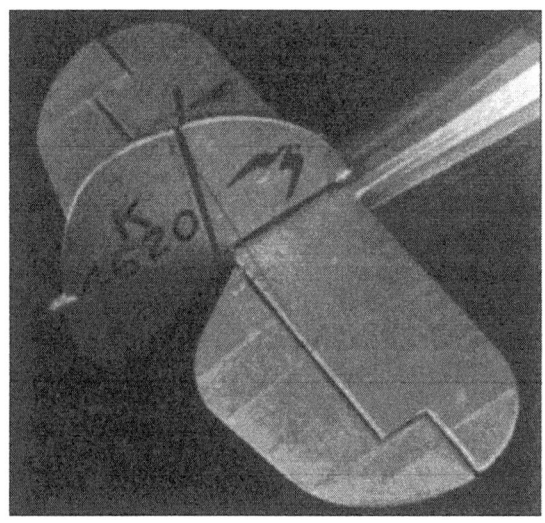

Even before covering, a tailplane made in this fashion is very stiff torsionally. When covered and doped a very strong and almost unwarpable unit is produced. Tail structures made this way are remarkably strong also in resisting 'edgeways-on' load such as frequently happen with fast downwind landings when the whole thing cartwheels.

When covered and doped a very realistic tail end is produced. The sheet sandwich forms an opaque centre to the structure preventing daylight shining through the thin surfaces when viewed in flight from below. The extremely thin leading and trailing edges are very apparent in these photographs.

I first saw such a sheet sandwich structure used on one of Jim Bridgewood's scale models, I think it must have been his Vigilant, at the 1952 Eddie Riding memorial competition held, as usual, at Woodford. I was competing with my then new DH 9a fitted with a conventional open-structured tailplane which had warped, of course! I don't know if Jim was the actual inventor of such a structure but I immediately cribbed it and built a new tailplane for the 9a in this manner and was an instant convert. I have used such structures ever since on all my scale models which includes the odd control liner as well as on radio models. I am amazed that such structures have not become more widely popular. Apart from my own immediate acquaintances in the Blackburn Aircraft, Doncaster and Lee Bees clubs, I don't know of any other modellers who have adopted this form of construction.

The elevators and rudder are attached to the tailplane and fin respectively by means of aluminium or tin fishplate type stiff hinges pushed into the centre of the spars adjacent to a wing rib (see Fig. 6.1).

The hinges should be stiff enough not to allow the inertia of the control surface to alter its setting during a heavy landing otherwise it will be virtually impossible to trim the model progressively. When the aeroplane is trimmed, it is desirable that the control surface is tack glued, using blobs of cement in the hinge line crack. If the setting has to be altered at a later date these can be cut through.

Wing structure

As mentioned previously, there are two basic types of wing structure: braced and cantilever. Invariably all braced structures are fabric covered and on most aeroplanes prior to about 1925, very thin in section. These wings are by far the most difficult to reproduce so that we have a strong, light, flexible structure that looks realistic.

Fig. 6.2 shows a typical undercambered wing section of a 1914–18 biplane. All sections of that period were very similar; some had more and some had less camber but invariably a considerable amount of undercamber was present. I personally always use the exact scale section for models of this period, making the wires do most of the work, but as mentioned in Chapter 3, a 20 per cent thickening of the section does not intrude very much and it allows deeper spars to be used.

When designing the wing, the first job is to work out the scantlings for the spars, which are usually dictated by the section itself. Virtually all biplanes have two spars and we have to adhere to their scale position to enable the interplane struts and wires to pick up on them. I used to use twin balsa spars notched into the upper and lower surfaces of the ribs which undoubtedly is the strongest and lightest method of sparring a wing, allowing the spars to

Figure 6.2. *Typical wing section 1914–18 aeroplane.*

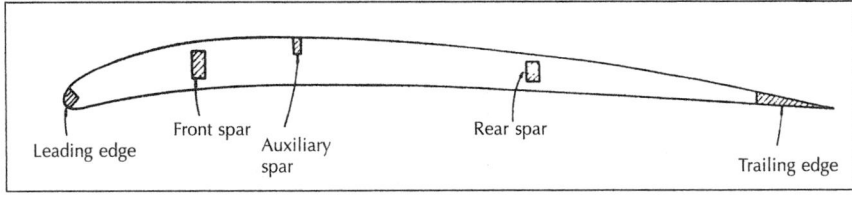

work farthest from the neutral axis. However, it is not very scale-like in appearance as the spars can clearly be seen when the wing is covered. In recent years I have used centrally disposed spars, as shown in Fig. 6.2. This is, of course, how spars are run in full-size practice so that they do not foul the covering. Although the covered wing looks much better, it is nothing like as efficient a structure and is also prone to elliptical dihedral warping. Because of the inefficiency of centrally disposed spars it is necessary to use spruce on all but the smallest models. At least $\frac{1}{16}$ in., and if possible a little more, of wing rib should traverse over and under the spars. Anything less and the ribs are too weak.

There is also a danger of the covering adhering to the spar where it sags between ribs. The best scantling you can then usually achieve is $\frac{1}{4}$ in. × $\frac{1}{8}$ in. for the front spar and $\frac{3}{16}$ in. × $\frac{1}{8}$ in. for the rear spar. These are quite adequate for a well-braced wing.

Elliptical dihedral warping is a problem to which I must confess I don't know the full answer. I think the cause is due to the asymmetric distribution of the spars (including the leading and trailing edges) in relation to tension in the covering. In other words because of the camber of the section all the spars are too low down; it certainly doesn't occur if the spars are on the wing surface as on the Rumpler. It is, of course, at its most marked if the spars are only on the lower surface. Terry Manley thought he had the answer when he fitted a third auxiliary spar, of $\frac{1}{8}$ in. × $\frac{1}{16}$ in. spruce, just below the surface at the point of maximum camber, as seen in Fig. 6.2, on the wings of his RE 8. I followed his example on my BE 12b. Neither of these models have been troubled with elliptical dihedral. However, on Terry's next model, the FK 8, he reported that the old trouble had occurred again despite this auxiliary spar.

I almost always use a light section leading edge, usually $\frac{1}{8}$ in. × $\frac{1}{8}$ in. balsa (set diamond wise). This is quite adequate with the close-set rib spacing prevailing.

I have not found a satisfactory answer to the trailing edge problem. Of course the originals were of a very light section but invariably internal wire bracing stiffened the structure. I have tried light sections, such as $\frac{3}{16}$ in. × $\frac{3}{32}$ in. spruce, but they have tended to warp badly locally. On large radio-controlled models, with chords in the region of 12in., it is possible to insert a thin sheet into the rear of the ribs and just cap the end, although with the thin trailing edges in the scales in which we are working, this is not very practical. All in all I find no alternative to the fairly large chord trailing edge of $\frac{1}{2}$ in. × $\frac{1}{8}$ in. or even $\frac{3}{4}$ in. × $\frac{1}{8}$ in. balsa, depending on the section. When the wing is painted and rib tapes are used, carrying the rib line to the extreme trailing edge, then the large section is hardly noticed. Do ensure that the trailing edge is accurately shaped to smoothly follow the contour of the ribs as any undulation in the wing section here is very noticeable.

Now to the manufacture of the ribs themselves. These should be cut from medium straight-grained $\frac{1}{16}$ in. or $\frac{1}{32}$ in. balsa. End ribs and the rear half ribs, at the aileron split, should be thicker ($\frac{1}{8}$ in. or $\frac{3}{16}$ in.) so that they do not pull in when the wing is covered and doped, $\frac{3}{16}$ in. thick being used if the section is very thin. Two templates are first cut from 16 swg or 14 swg dural plate complete with all notches and cutouts for spars. In order to make the rectangular holes for the two spars, a $\frac{1}{8}$ in. diameter hole is first drilled and the rectangle opened out with a $\frac{3}{32}$ in. square file.

Two random $\frac{1}{32}$ in. holes are made in the template for pins, between the front spar and leading edge and the rear spar and trailing edge. Rectangles of sheet, slightly larger than the templates, are then cut and sandwiched between the templates. The whole bundle is then pinned together and the ribs carved and sanded to the contours of the template. Each wing set is made individually. This means we have a bundle of about 20 ribs at each go, i.e. $1\frac{1}{4}$

My Leopard Moth seen before the leading edge sheeting was applied. I also used a full-depth spar on these wings as this was the simplest answer to a problem created by the large span ailerons and inboard flaps – very little fixed surface extends beyond this spar.

WING AND TAILPLANE CONSTRUCTION

in. thick if $\frac{1}{16}$ in. sheet is used. (With average spacing I usually use $\frac{1}{16}$ in. ribs but for closer spaced jobs there are advantages in using $\frac{1}{32}$ in. First, the weight saving. This is not as great as might be at first thought, as a harder grade of balsa must be used for the thinner ribs if they are to resist buckling. The greatest advantage is that more can be sandwiched together between templates at one go, so reducing the rib-making chore!) Before the bundle of ribs are separated the spar holes are cut, again using the $\frac{1}{8}$ in. drill, which is run in from each side, and the $\frac{3}{32}$ in. square file. Check that a section of spar will pass through the bundle of ribs before separating. The spar should be a fairly loose fit in its tunnel of holes.

I always make my ailerons separately, but each at the same time as its respective wing panel. This means that the outboard ribs require cutting and a piece removed to allow for the aileron spar. To achieve this I usually cut one of the templates to the correct length to cater for the aileron spar and use this as a pattern for shortening the required number of ribs. Similarly if riblets are required (and they usually are – in their hundreds!) the front portion of one of the templates is cut to the length of a riblet and used as a pattern. I am afraid that riblets are too small, usually, to block together so that they have to be individually cut out with a balsa knife – to me the most hateful job in all aeromodelling! Of course it is possible to choose a prototype without riblets; the Rumpler CV is one and the White Falcon another. The latter offers a double bonus in that it doesn't have ailerons either, having wing warping instead.

Having cut and shaped all our spars and ribs, we are now ready to commence assembly. The trailing edge is first pinned down on the plan, taking care to pack up the front by the correct amount to cater for the undercamber. With undercambered wings I always find it an advantage to notch the front of the trailing edge spar about $\frac{1}{16}$ in. to receive the ribs. I know this is bad practice structurally, but it does make assembly very much easier. It is unnecessary with a flat-bottomed section as the trailing edge of the rib is resting hard against the building board. All the ribs are now slotted onto the two spars and their trailing edges glued into their respective notches in the trailing edge spar. Each rib is pinned to the plan at its nose and the leading edge glued in place. The aileron is built packing the aileron spar up the correct amount so that the split ribs line up correctly.

If a $\frac{1}{8}$ in. × $\frac{1}{16}$ in. spruce anti-warp spar is to be fitted, it should be let in to the upper surface of the ribs at the point of maximum camber (see Fig. 6.2). At this point the ribs should be slotted $\frac{1}{16}$ in. × $\frac{3}{16}$ in. deep. (This is slotted in the template and cut out of the ribs when they are blocked together.) The $\frac{1}{8}$ in. × $\frac{1}{16}$

in. spar is the last to be fitted and is dropped down to the bottom of the slot, leaving a $\frac{1}{16}$ in. gap on top. This gap is filled by bits of $\frac{1}{16}$ in. square to give a smooth top rib contour.

The wing tips now follow. Their construction of course varies according to the shape. Square tips are relatively simple and can follow normal methods as on the White Falcon wing. If a rounded form is to be built, however, it is best built along the lines of the tailplane. The spars can be slotted outboard of the last rib, or even the penultimate rib if a stronger job would result, and $\frac{1}{32}$ in. sheet let in. This should be pre-curved to the necessary camber of the tip. This is a point often overlooked – flat tips on a highly cambered wing look hideous. The top half of the tip section, usually $\frac{3}{32}$ in. square, is then pre-curved, by the usual technique, and glued in place. When the structure is set the wing is unpinned and removed from the plan, and the lower half of the tip section is then added. Strips of $\frac{1}{16}$ in. $\times$ $\frac{1}{8}$ in. (or thicker if required) are added above and below the rear spar adjacent to the aileron spar. The various hard points are then added as well as the ply end facing rib. The whole wing structure is then thoroughly sanded, particular care being given to the wing tips. As with the tail end, this form of structure will take a lot of end-on punishment and wing tips get plenty of that! The photograph of my BE 12b wing tip undergoing repair is an interesting case. The $\frac{1}{32}$ in. sheet should have been carried back to the penultimate rib but I am afraid I was rather lazy and only sheeted outboard of the last rib. The resultant structure is obviously weak in the vicinity of the front spar. During a heavy cartwheeling landing the whole tip section, between the spars, was stoved in. As can be seen a compromise modification was made by inserting a prop midway between the spars, between the two most outboard ribs.

To return to our typical wing construction, all that now remains to do is to fit the various interplane strut and wire attachments to the structure (these points were covered extensively in the previous chapter). Finally the innermost pair of ribs are drilled to take either the brass tubes or the dowels and these items glued to the ribs and spars. A check should be made that each wing panel accurately lines up on the fuselage, or centre section, at the correct incidence angle before the epoxy glue sets.

Wings on post-war (i.e. 1914–18) biplanes and monoplanes are generally easier to construct, due to their thicker section. Very often they were sheeted with ply between the leading edge and the front spar, to form a box spar. The front spar is usually nearer to the leading edge than was the practice during the war years, to facilitate this. On smallish models, around 36in. span, I generally reproduce this box spar out of solid medium balsa. I have done this

WING AND TAILPLANE CONSTRUCTION

The BE 12's wing tip undergoing repairs as detailed in the text. Laziness was the reason for the damage – if the sheeting had been continued to the next rib the model may have escaped unscathed. A rectangle of $\frac{1}{32}$ in. sheet between the last two ribs and the front and rear spars would have been better than the short strut shown.

An unusual subject is D. P. Golding's Hawker Hornbill, only 25 in. span, originally E. D. Baby – powered but later flown with a D. C. Merlin. Wing spars are let into the lower surface of each wing, giving chance of warps.

Apart from the short nose, which causes rearward centre of gravity problems, the Avro Tutor is a fine subject – this example belonging to the Shuttleworth Collection. The ability to inspect the full size is most important to the competition-minded builder. Note cabane and squared-off tips, plus aileron connector strut.

on the Hawker Nimrod and also the Bucker Jüngmann, the scantling of the latter being $\frac{5}{16}$ in. deep × $\frac{1}{2}$ in. wide. With a hefty spar like this at the front you can cut back a little on the scantlings of the remainder. However, a rear spar is still needed to carry the rear interplane strut and wires. On the Jüngmann this was on the lower surface of the wing, the heavy leading edge allowing me to get away with this to a large extent. However, on the Nimrod I put it in the middle and I think this is the best place for it. On the Jüngmann I used a small section spruce trailing edge which, as I stated earlier, I do not now recommend.

For larger models with box leading edges, a built-up section should be used which follows traditional lines, i.e. small section leading edge, upper and lower front spars and $\frac{1}{16}$ in. leading edge sheeting.

That concludes the treatise on wing structure with the exception of the reproduction of the all-ply covered and stressed skin wings. Aeroplanes with wing structure of this form are generally not very suitable prototypes for free-flight models. Much has been written on this type of construction, usually using foam wing cores, in the specialist radio-control model publications in recent years and, therefore, I shall not repeat it all again here.

CHAPTER 7

Covering and Finishing

The last three chapters have dealt almost exclusively with the structure of free-flight scale models. I realise that I have far from covered all aspects of construction which has altered considerably in recent years, but have dealt in greatest detail with the structure which is most peculiar to this class of model, and biplanes in particular, because I feel that this is where most people, or their models, come unstuck. I could go on indefinitely about scale model structures but I think now is the time to look at covering the airframe.

Having completed the structure of a scale model and rigged it, it always seems such a shame to cover up so much of your handiwork. I have known modellers who, in fact, cannot bear to proceed beyond this stage and leave their models naked for years! I usually allow myself a week of such indulgence during which time I take a picture or two and weigh the thing. Large clatter from kitchen scales and a shudder down the spine when you realise that you have only got $\frac{1}{2}$oz left for covering, doping, detail and 3oz of lead in the nose to balance it if you are to make your target weight!

As stated before, the covering of full-sized aeroplanes falls into three categories: fabric, plywood and metal (painted or unpainted). Most aeroplanes are a combination of two materials. Early aircraft were usually a combination of plywood and fabric, while between the wars aluminium sheet replaced the plywood and in the last 50 years has replaced the fabric also. However, most of the subjects suitable for free flight have large areas fabric covered, the flying surfaces almost entirely so, which is just as well as fabric is the lightest, and by far the cheapest form of covering to simulate.

Irrespective of the size of the model I recommend only one form of covering to represent fabric: lightweight Jap silk laid over lightweight Modelspan tissue. Up to, and including, my $1\frac{1}{2}$ Strutter built in 1959, I used paper only for covering purposes – lightweight Modelspan for models up to about 36in. span and heavyweight Modelspan for larger machines. Tissue on

SCALE AIRCRAFT FOR FREE FLIGHT

Vic Driscoll of St. Albans flew this magnificent free-flight Westland Wapiti so impressively it became the clear winner of its class in the 1971 All-Scale Rally held at Old Warden. It weighs 30oz and uses a Marown Snipe 1.5cc diesel.

its own is not an ideal covering for scale models; although light and easily filled with dope it is not very strong and becomes brittle with age so that holes and splits are forever appearing. As the model becomes more and more patched it soon looks more like a well-worn duration model than a scale model. I then experimented with nylon and silk. The former is suitable for models around 6ft span, i.e. scale radio models, on which is it used extensively, but falls down on three counts when used on the size of model we are interested in. First, it is too heavy, particularly when filled with dope, for which it has a greater thirst than modellers have for beer! Secondly, it doesn't like bending around sharp corners of which we have plenty and thirdly, its weave is too coarse to represent Irish linen reduced to around 1/12th scale. It is, however, immensely strong. My next experiments were with Japanese silk used on its own. This I found to be ideal in fineness of weave and also very light and flexible, although unfortunately it is hardly stronger than lightweight Modelspan, being very prone to splitting.

COVERING AND FINISHING

It was about this time that I had a long discussion with John Simmance, in a hut at Linton-on-Ouse one wet Northern Gala, during the judging of the Selby Trophy event which the Northern Area used to run for free-flight scale models in the 1960s. I had always admired John's finishes and was amazed at how well his covering stood up to the battering which his far-from-lightweight models received. It was then that John let me into the secret of the 'silk on Modelspan' technique he used. I tried it out on my next model, a Blackburn Airedale, and found it to be very successful, which is more than can be said for the Airedale, which absolutely refused to fly – my only total failure in some 20 years or more! Nevertheless, it proved the covering technique for me. Both Terry Manley and myself have used it exclusively for all our scale models ever since. It is lighter than heavyweight Modelspan (with the usual four coats of dope necessary to eliminate that hairy-spider effect) and far stronger. The lightweight Modelspan underlay completely eliminates any tendency to split under normal loading.

Before describing the covering technique in detail, a word or two about the materials. Scale models use dope in copious quantities. I always use *Titanine Clear Glider Dope* to specification MA3. This is fairly thick stuff which I thin to various degrees for different applications. I always buy it in gallon tins which works out much cheaper than half pint tins. The only time I use it at full strength is for adhesive purposes, when attaching the Modelspan to the airframe. I know a lot of people have trouble with doping tissue on and prefer to use paste but I would recommend perseverance with the use of dope

The Nexus Plans Service plan for the VA Walrus (FSP 661) has always been a popular challenge. This fine example was at the 1971 All-Scale Rally, Old Warden, among R. Hibbert's collection from Coventry.

because once it is mastered it is a far superior method, giving a neater bond, without lumps and, what is more, not impairing the strength of the tissue when in contact; allowing it to be pulled around more to eliminate tip wrinkles.

Lightweight Modelspan hardly requires any description – it has been the standard covering material since the last war, despite a couple of periods when manufacture apparently ceased. For our purposes white is the chosen colour because the silk is available in white these days and we invariably paint over it. Try to buy it uncreased, but if this is impossible iron it before use.

Lightweight Japanese silk appears to be available in spurts. Quite often it is impossible to obtain for months on end and then everybody stocks it. It is advisable, therefore, to hold a couple of yards or so in stock. The price is pretty astronomic but not a vast amount is needed, it will last a long time and functionally and visually it has no equal. Again iron out creases before use.

Now for the covering in detailed stages:

(1) Break the model down into as many components as possible, i.e. de-rig and separate ailerons from wings, and elevators from tailplane etc.
(2) Apply two coats of 50 per cent thinned dope to the entire airframe, sanding after each to smooth out any swelling of the grain. If there are extensive areas of sheet balsa give these a third coat.
(3) Cover the entire model with lightweight Modelspan preferably using dope as the adhesive. Stick the tissue to each piece of structure, in particular undercambered wing ribs. Cover all sheeted areas as well as areas to be 'silked' as this strengthens the sheet covering tremendously. Lap all edges of tissue over. Cover complex curves on rounded fuselages and wing tips with several small pieces to avoid wrinkles.
(4) Dope the entire airframe with 75 per cent strength dope. With good dope at high strength, water shrinking is unnecessary. If the structure has been made on the lines described in previous chapters there is no need to pin down, which I regard as a terrible chore anyway!
(5) Give the fuselage a second coat of dope at 50 per cent strength.
(6) Lightly sand entire airframe.
(7) If parts of the fuselage are sheeted and are to be painted without any form of overlay covering, such as metal foil, then these should be filled at this stage before applying the silk to the rest of the fuselage. I find a couple of coats of *Belco Primer Surfacer* usually does the job. This material contains lead however, and is rather heavy so confine it to the nose end only. I find this form of filler far better than proprietary sanding sealers which tend to be greasy and give a poor key for colour dopes. They are also prone to cracking.

Before and after views of my 1/12th scale Hawker Nimrod show the model as it was test flown (top) when just covered and 'metal-skinned', and in its final form after these tests proved satisfactory. This scheme may indicate lack of confidence, but it saves work if the worst is apparent.

(8) Now for the application of the silk. I have tried many ways but find the following the best. It may seem a little tricky at first but you soon get the hang of it. Silk is much more flexible than tissue and will cover more compound curves without resorting to nicking, which always looks unsightly. A pair of really sharp scissors are essential for cutting silk: it is worthwhile investing in a new pair and keeping them for this job. That old pair most modellers possess, which double for tinsnips, are not really good enough. Carefully cut the silk to the shape required with about $\frac{1}{2}$in. overlap. Lay the silk over the tissue-covered surface dry and smooth down as close as possible. The electrostatic effect will tend to pull the silk down close. With a soft camel-haired mop, brush 50 per cent thinned dope through the silk. Start in the centre of the area and work out to the extremities, taking care to avoid trapped air 'bells'. Elimination of air

Another advocate of 'painting when proved' is J. Turvey, seen here test gliding his unpainted Sopwith $1\frac{1}{2}$ Strutter, built to 1/12th scale and powered by a Mills .75cc.

bells is the reason for ironing the silk and smoothing it down dry. If you try the traditional double-covering technique of doping the Modelspan and then laying on the silk you get in a hopeless mess because silk saturated in dope is virtually impervious to air. Cover all undersurfaces first and trim with a slight overlap. If any air bells have formed under the silk then nick the silk, but not the Modelspan, with a sharp balsa knife and push dope into the bell with a brush. Smooth the offending silk down with the fingers.

(9) If the subject is a WWI machine, we don't want a smooth finish on the silk, therefore a further coat of dope, at 25 per cent strength, is all that should be applied on top of the silk. The edges of surfaces are then lightly sanded and a further coat of 50 per cent strength dope applied at the edges only to obviate the hairy look. If the subject is of a later vintage, with a better fabric finish, then two coats of 50 per cent strength dope can be applied all over.

It is now worthwhile rigging the model again and checking that everything lines up OK. The tail surfaces can be permanently attached at this stage.

Although far from complete and looking very plain in its off-white finish, the model is now in a condition in which it can be flown. I always test fly my models at this stage because of a number of advantages: the model is much lighter than when complete with all paintwork and details and, therefore, is less likely to damage itself in the first crucial trimming flights. If you are unfortunate enough to damage it at this stage, and let's face it the risk is rather high, then it is a much simpler task to repair and disguise with paint later.

Finally if the thing just will not fly, or you write it off completely, you have not wasted your time painting and making all the fiddly details which can account for 50 per cent of the time expended on the model. Trimming and flying is dealt with later.

Assuming that we have successfully completed our trimming flights we can return to finishing the model off with great encouragement knowing we have a flying proposition, or alternatively throw it to one side and start looking for a more suitable prototype! A heart-breaking decision, but worth making rather than waste time finishing it. To me if the model cannot be made to fly, a bonfire is a better death than a dust-collecting ornament.

Applying the finish

Before painting, two more steps should be taken, or at least considered – rib tapes and control horns. Rib tapes are only worthwhile, in my opinion, on larger machines, above 36in. span. Their purpose on the full-sized machine is to cover up the lacing of the fabric to the ribs. More fastidious radio scale modellers are now simulating stitching beneath the tapes as well, but it is hardly practical on the scales we are working at. Baby ribbon is the standard material for rib tapes on large radio models, although unfortunately I have not been able to obtain narrow enough tape for a free-flight model as $\frac{1}{8}$in. to $\frac{3}{16}$in. width is what we are interested in. I always cut my own from heavyweight Modelspan and am fortunate in having access to a drawing office shear for this purpose, which soon reduces a sheet of paper literally to shreds. The hard way to do it is to use a steel straight edge and razor blade. The tapes are doped on top, and beneath, each rib and riblet. When colour is applied to the wing the effect is well worthwhile. Continuing the rib line to the absolute trailing edge of the wing masks the necessary heavy spar at that point.

Control horns are best made from 20 swg or 22 swg light alloy (not soft aluminium) – I have made them from plywood in the past and sometimes still do for the tail surfaces if I am critical on weight at the back end. Aileron horns in ply are hopeless as the lower ones get ground away due to wing tips scraping the concrete and the upper ones break during nose-overs. Do not attach the control wires to the horns until after painting.

If metal panels which are to be painted are part of the fuselage they should be added now. If the panels are to be left in their natural state then they are best fitted later.

One last thing before applying the colour. Draw in the outer circles (or crosses/or whatever) of the insignia with a soft pencil and paint up to the line.

There is nothing worse than trying to paint white over camouflage green, especially when the green starts to leach through.

Now a word about paints. I personally always use cellulose, well thinned and brushed on with a good quality camel or sable-haired brush about $\frac{3}{4}$ in. wide. You will have to pay a fair amount for a good one so look after it by washing it in thinners immediately after use. While on the subject of brushes you will also want a No. 5 for general paint work and a No. 0 for lettering. These are best bought at an artists' shop. The average brush sold for a few pence at model shops is useless for our purpose unless of course you admire hairs laid all over your models. Good brushes will last for years with proper care – I have had my main doping mop for at least 15 years. To get back to paint, I find nothing superior to cellulose for either a matt or a gloss finish. As we are not using 'hot' fuels, a fuel proofer is not necessary. Matt cellulose is obtainable from Marcel Guest Ltd. of Collyhurst, Manchester. A word of warning here regarding plastic enamel, which is freely available. Matt plastic enamel is not diesel fuel proof, and over a long period it goes sticky with a horrible mess ensuing. The gloss enamel seems proof enough but it takes an age to dry between coats if you want to rub down. If you are compelled to use a glow motor as the radio fraternity are, then matt polyurethane varnish over

My DH 9A seen immediately after its trimming session. Note the unfinished condition – the rear end is completed while the more vulnerable parts are yet to be painted.

cellulose produces a semi-matt finish which is reasonably fuel proof, but I would recommend something harder in the region of the engine bay. Another alternative is provided by Humbrol Ltd., who produce a matt fuel proofer especially for the scale modeller, packed in their familiar and convenient tinlets, or even in a spray pack.

Our silk-covered surface is still pretty porous so that two thinned coats of matt khaki dope effectively covers a typical WWI job. These machines were invariably left clear doped underneath and after much experimentation I have come to the conclusion this is best reproduced in a similar manner on a model, i.e. leave it alone. Perhaps a few streaks from a brush dipped in dirty thinners adds to the realism. Certainly cream dope, which so many people apply, looks completely wrong; many aeroplanes stored in museums have gone that way due to the varnish yellowing with age, but they never look like cream paint!

If the prototype was left in natural fabric all over then I am afraid clear doped silk looks far too stark. Both Terry Manley on his Vimy, and myself, on my Blackburn White Falcon experimented with a coat of magnolia emulsion paint, on top of the Modelspan, before applying the silk. Although they looked better than with undoped silk, they still did not look quite right. The best advice I can offer is to avoid unpainted prototypes – they get very dirty and look shabby very quickly anyway!

After khaki, silver is the next most popular colour, being almost universal for between-wars military aircraft. Thin the silver dope and keep it well stirred as the metallic particles soon settle out. Three or four thinned coats are usually adequate.

That leaves us with the gloss colours used on civilian machines. Here a case can certainly be made for spraying and anyone who has access to professional spraying equipment would be well advised to use it. Unfortunately I have no contact in the spraying business and so continue with the back of the camel, which I find infinitely superior to the cheap little hand sprayers. Some colours go on better than others – blues, greens and reds are OK but yellow and white can be tricky. They must be used very thin and up to eight coats may be necessary to get a good depth of colour. Wet rubbing down over sheet surfaces is recommended between coats.

The next job is to apply the decorations, my term for roundels, squadron markings, serial numbers, registration letters etc. Forget transfers – they look crude and come off in time.

Roundels are easy. Use a pair of ink compasses loaded with the correct coloured dope. Use a brush to load the pen, never dip it into the jar. Keep the

Rather a contrast to my approach is Andy MacIsaac's $\frac{3}{4}$ in. : 1ft Hawker Fury. This has scale rib spacing, scale tail surfaces and landing gear, and slightly increased dihedral. The cowl and wheels are vacuum-formed plastic. This model gained top scale points for the second year running in the Indoor Scale section of the 1971 US Nationals.

dope well thinned and keep washing the pen in thinners. Tape a piece of card to the wing at the centre of the roundel for the compass point to bear on, then draw inner and outer circles of each colour and fill in with the No. 5 brush. Always start with the white.

Mask as much of the rest of the decorations as possible: the diamonds on the upper surfaces of my Nimrod are a typical masking job. With regard to

High-wing cabin monoplanes are usually ideal prototypes and often have bright, attractive colour schemes. This $\frac{1}{10}$ scale Rearwin 6000M Speedster, 30 ozs, Cox ·049 engine, was Edward Fort's 1971 US Nats entry.

COVERING AND FINISHING

the serial numbers I am afraid there is no alternative to painstaking signwriting. I always draw the outlines of the figures onto the surface first with a very soft pencil, a 4B being ideal. I then fill in, with dope, using the No. 0 brush. When the dope is dry, a soft rubber removes the pencil marks but make sure it is dry though! For very small lettering of the 'lift here' variety I think it is best to revert to *Letraset*.

Finally in this chapter I wish to deal with simulated metal panelling. For deep compound curves, such as are found on noses of in-line engine fighters, there is no option but to beat the panels, cowlings etc., out of soft aluminium if we want a natural metallic finish and I will cover metal bashing in the next section. A simple alternative is to select a painted prototype and carve the difficult curves from balsa wood, although admittedly silver-painted wood is no substitute for polished metal for anything but the smallest areas. For areas which have only mild compound curves, and this is usually the major part, I can recommend *Metalskin*. This is sold at most shops which specialise in the more exotic plastic models – the ones which run radio outfits a close second in price! It is not cheap but is worth it compared with aluminium foil such as *Bacofoil* because it is self-adhesive when you peel away the backing paper. This is a great boon because I find it extremely difficult to get an impact

D. P. Golding's 38in. span Fairey Fox powered by a Mills 1.3cc. This model illustrates the high standard of construction with the builder showing preference for 'non-working' rigging (i.e. shirring elastic), as well as spars let into the lower surface of the ribs only (not in accordance with my views).

adhesive to lie smoothly under foil. Double curvature is applied by 'spooning' on the reverse side before removing the backing, while rivets can be simulated by embossing from the reverse side. Each individual panel should be cut and shaped prior to attachment to the model. Even on completely flat areas do not try to cover in one large sheet and score out the panels later.*

For flat areas it is cheaper to use metal stencil plates. These are bonded to paper making the adhesion job very much easier, PVA or an impact adhesive being ideal. Of course, thin sheet aluminium can also be used but this is rarely available in thin enough sheets to avoid a big weight penalty. Terry Manley specialises in this form of plating, as can be seen from the close-up of the FK 8. However, he has access to a chemical etching plant which reduces his aluminium down to a few thou. It also imparts a nice scale satin sheen to the surface.

Even if you intend to paint the model all over I think it is worth panelling in metal as it adds to the realism enormously, especially if you scratch the paint away a bit, here and there, particularly at the edges and corners with fine wet and dry paper. The BE 12b has received this 'treatment' and it looks very authentic and 'battle worn'.

One final point on natural metal finishes. Always apply two coats of clear dope over the *Metalskin* etc., to seal the edges and cracks, otherwise fuel will creep under and attack the adhesive, allowing the panel to lift.

---

*"Metalskin" is apparently nowadays known as "Bare Metal Foil", produced by a manufacturer of the same name – Ed.

CHAPTER 8

Detail

Without doubt, the accuracy and skill with which the detailed parts are executed decides whether the model looks like a realistic replica or just a toy aeroplane. I have seen the most beautifully constructed scale models, with unblemished finishes, from which the air of realism was completely lacking due, I am sure, to a lack of suitable attention to detail. This has been noticeable even at World Championships where, with the exception of the top models, the gleaming new toy image has sometimes been most apparent. Aeroplanes in service, particularly wartime military service, rapidly become very shabby as reference to photographs in the files of the Imperial War Museum photographic library will reveal. Paint scratched or eroded away, dents, and ill-fitting cowlings are all very much in evidence.

Now I would be the last to uphold the BE as a shining example of scale model craftsmanship (it was built far too quickly for that) but it does possess an air of realism, both on the ground and in the air, that many scale models,

Terry Manley's Armstrong FK8 (which won the Super Scale Trophy at the 1971 Nationals) uses a chemically etched aluminium cowl – rather beyond the average enthusiast's resources though! The etched finish imparts a nice sheen to the aluminium.

The most fascinating part of my modelling is trying to exude 'character' from my subjects. Here the chipped paint over metal panelling generates a really worn 'in-service' look.

on which many more hours have obviously been spent, fail to capture. It is very difficult to put into words just how the air of realism is achieved. Obviously it takes time spread over a number of models and you cannot expect to achieve it 100 per cent first time. However, in this chapter I intend to discuss the major details at some length and explain what I think is the best way to reproduce them in a manner suitable for a free-flight model where, as ever, weight is of paramount importance.

For the sake of convenience we will start at the nose and work our way back to the tail. This is not necessarily the order in which you should go about the job. This can only be decided by the builder and, of course, is dictated somewhat by the nature of the prototype. In fact, quite a lot of detail work should be carried out before the painting operation and as mentioned in the last chapter I would recommend test flying the model before any detail work whatsoever is commenced.

Propellers

It is usually quite impossible for the motor in a scale model to operate with a scale propeller. Even though the good old long-stroke Mills engine may swing a propeller of scale diameter it almost certainly cannot turn one of such fearsome pitch and blade area used by vintage aeroplanes at anything like the revolutions necessary to fly the model. We, therefore, need two propellers, one for flying and one for scale appearance. The flying prop can be any of the proprietary brands, preferably nylon, about 3in. to 4in. pitch and as large a

— DETAIL —

diameter as the engine will swing, but not exceeding scale diameter of course.

We shall have to make our scale propeller. Even if we do not intend to enter scale contests, for which a scale propeller is essential for static judging, this is a worthwhile exercise even if just for the photographs. Most of the propellers on the aeroplanes in which we are interested were made of laminated wood. Sometimes this was left uncovered and varnished – very common on 1914–18 machines – or covered with fabric and doped, which was usually the case on later aeroplanes. Very few metal propellers were used before the Second World War. If our prototype has a fabric-covered propeller we are in easy street. Just carve one from a lump of suitable hardwood – mahogany, beech or birch are ideal – and paint accordingly. For a small model, laminated props can be made from compressed laminated wood which goes under the name of *Jabroc* or *Hydulignum*. Its most common use these days is for press tools

Close-up of the lower wing tip of my BE 12b shows the 'natural finish' of silk applied over lightweight tissue, as discussed in Chapter 7, and the hand-painted roundel – none of your super-glossy transfers here! Note also the aluminium aileron horn and the effect of the rib tapes.

This ambitious Manley creation is a Vickers Vimy Atlantic utilising two Mills .75cc engines and to approximately 1/16th scale. The model is painted overall with magnolia emulsion paint, while the cowlings are once more chemically etched aluminium. Twin-engined free-flight scale models are not for the inexperienced or weak-hearted!

and rubber die presses used for forming light alloy in the aircraft industry. It cannot be carved, but it can be efficiently worked with a rasp, finishing with glasspaper and it takes a lovely polish. Unfortunately the laminations are too close-pitched for any but the smallest scales. A propeller was usually made from between six and eight laminations. Therefore, for larger models, of around 1/10 scale, we shall have to lay our own blank up from laminations of mahogany, about $\frac{1}{10}$ in. thick, just like the real thing. Use a good wood glue such as *Aerolite* and clamp while setting, then carve as per a solid prop. The result is very rewarding.

Most propellers had metal capping, usually brass, on their leading edges. On small props this can be represented by brassy paint (gold plus grey). But

The Blackburn White Falcon is also finished with the magnolia emulsion technique. This model was built by me in 1971 to 1/12th scale and powered by a faithful Mills .75cc.

— DETAIL —

again on larger props genuine brass sheathing looks far better. The final finishing touch is in the hub. A centre plate is cut from either brass or light alloy and the lightening holes, if any, drilled. Nuts of the appropriate size are epoxied to the disc (as can be seen in the photograph of the BE), and the whole epoxied to the front of the propeller. Usually the scale hub is of greater thickness than the amount of crankshaft projecting from the driving plate, therefore the scale propeller can just be a push fit onto the crankshaft.

Cowls

I suppose this item causes more anguish than any other in scale model construction. I am sure more scale prototypes are rejected because of the difficulty of reproducing the cowl, or the exposed engine because of the lack of one, than any other feature. If all cowls were as simple as the AW FK 8 we would be laughing!

Cowls can be made of any, or a combination of, three materials: aluminium, wood or glass fibre. Aluminium is the strongest, the best and essential if it is to remain unpainted. However, it is undoubtedly the most difficult to work. It is relatively simple when double curvature is not present and foil can be glued over a sheet balsa surface, as described in Chapter 7. For a removable part such as a cowl top, as on the BE, it is a simple matter to bend and cut a piece of 22 swg or 24 swg aluminium plate to shape. While on the subject of

The nose of my BE 12b – note the general 'war worn' look with paint scratched and dirty exhaust pipes. The cylinder bank cowls are moulded from acetate sheet and the aluminium disc on the dummy propeller has nuts epoxied on.

SCALE AIRCRAFT FOR FREE FLIGHT

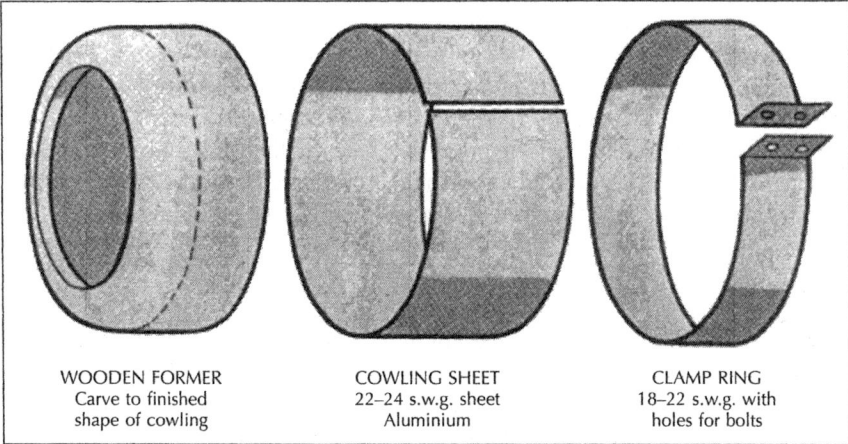

WOODEN FORMER	COWLING SHEET	CLAMP RING
Carve to finished	22–24 s.w.g. sheet	18–22 s.w.g. with
shape of cowling	Aluminium	holes for bolts

Figure 8.1. *The only special tools needed to make a circular aluminium cowling are the wooden former and a clamp ring. Cut the material to be used in a strip long enough to wrap right round the block, and approximately $\frac{1}{2}$ in. wider than the total cowl width. Bend this strip around a suitable object 1 in. smaller in diameter than the hardwood pattern so that it finally fits close to the pattern, with the edges just meeting.*

removable cowls, I find the neatest and quickest way of retention is by means of a large press-stud fastener of the type used on some types of battery. Solder a strip of tin to the backs of both the male and female parts of the stud and then epoxy one half to the underside of the cowl and the other half to a structure, built up from the bearers, so as to allow the two halves of the fastener to mate when the cowl is tight home. The strips of tin are essential to give a large enough area for the epoxy to take the load. If you try to glue the press stud directly to the cowl it will pull off the first time you remove the cowl.

To get back to aluminium cowl manufacture. Any degree of double curvature will require form blocks to be made. A male block is the simplest and should be carved from suitable hardwood to the finished size of the cowl less the metal thickness, usually 22 swg. Probably the most common cowling shape we are called upon to reproduce is the circular job used to surround the rotary engines of the WWI period or the radials of a later period. The form block for these is best produced on a lathe but can be carved if this luxury is not available. The various stages of bashing the metal to the shape we require are illustrated in Figs 8.2 to 8.7. All other forms of double curvature can be beaten in a similar manner, with a suitable block and a fair amount of patience. Sometimes it is necessary to 'lose' metal as the shape is formed. This is best done by judicious nicks in the area of superfluity. These are not

─── DETAIL ───

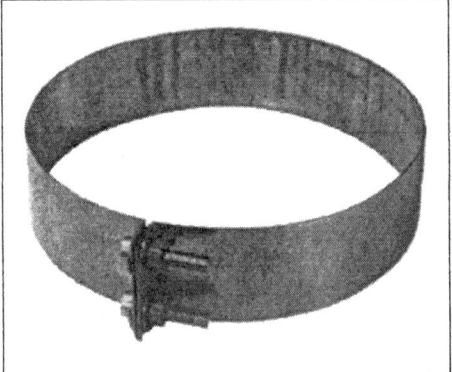

Figure 8.2. Turn or carve the hardwood pattern to the final cowl shape required, less the thickness of the aluminium sheet. **Figure 8.3.** Make a clamp ring from heavier gauge material allowing for the final diameter. Make as deep as possible.

noticeable when the job is finished and polished. If access to an aluminium welding facility is available then the nicks can be welded, prior to polishing, for a stronger job. With regard to materials always use aluminium and not light alloy which is far too hard to work. The aluminium should be normalised before working. A simple way to do this is to rub soap over the metal and heat, either by means of a blowlamp or a gas ring, until the soap

Figure 8.4. Using a small ball pein hammer, beat the aluminium from the outside towards the centre with the clamp ring bolted firmly in position. **Figure 8.5.** Without the clamp ring, the job would look like this. There is no need for concern – just keep tapping it to shape, gradually folding the top edge over.

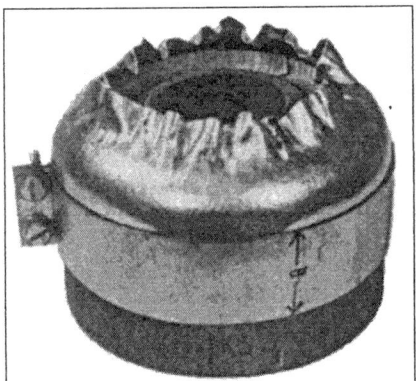
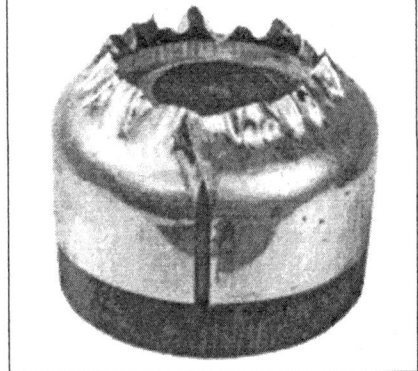

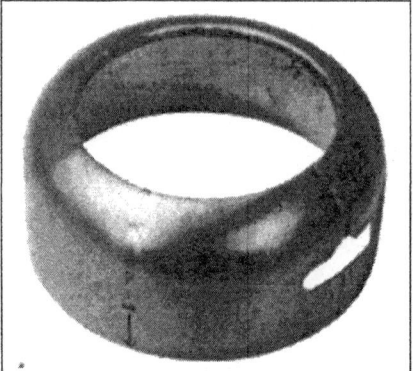 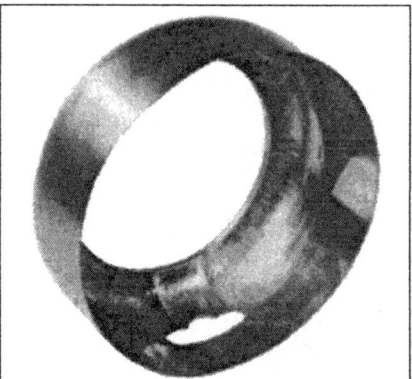

Figure 8.6. Polish all the hammer marks off with a fine buffing wheel, or by hand with an emery cloth. Trim all edges including the join seam. **Figure 8.7.** Finish the seam off with a patch of aluminium epoxied to the inside. Give a final polish if the cowl is to be left 'natural'.

has turned black all over, then quench in cold water. The soap is used merely as a temperature indicator; it does not impart magical softening qualities to the metal. During beating you may find that the metal-work hardens. A further normalising treatment at this stage will make the going much easier. A hide mallet rather than a hammer should be used for beating.

Wooden cowls do not require much to be said about them. They are, of course, by far the easiest to make but generally balsa wood is not a satisfactory material. Being at the front end, its one major attribute, weight, is of no advantage. Its soft surface is soon damaged by a nose-scraper landing

This Blackburn White Falcon, built by me to 1/12th scale in 1971, is 40in. span and powered by the faithful Mills .75 – the cylinder head can just be seen lurking in the bulkhead area above the detailed dummy rotary engine. Construction of those distinctive wheels is covered in the text.

——————————————— DETAIL ———————————————

A Blackburn Ripon built by me in 1958 to 1/12th scale. This uses a glass fibre cowl which is very strong – you do not need any skill with a hammer to produce one of these!

which I am afraid occurs all too often on a free-flight model. Balsa is best used, where applicable, as a core material on which some other harder material such as metal is laid. In this form it does an excellent job in stabilising the engine bearers. Where balsa is used 'naked' it should be extremely well filled, using primer surfacer, before painting. This will give it a polished metal look – when new at any rate!

The other material for cowls which has come into fairly general use is fibreglass. The cowlings of my Ripon and the Rumpler CV, both built in the 1950s, were of this material but I must admit I have not used it recently. This is more because the cowls of models I have made in the last few years have lent themselves to other methods. Although the actual fabrication of the glass

The RE 8 has a typical semi-enclosed engine installation, in this case an RAF V12. J. Moreley's model is most realistic with the engine cylinders having 'wound wire' fins, pressed aluminium exhaust pipes and a simple bent aluminium hood.

The nose of Terry Manley's AW FK 8 reveals simple slab-sided cowl shape 'plated' with thin dural on top of balsa sheet. The realistic radiator is formed from brass epoxied together.

fibre cowl is relatively easy, the preparation of the mould is a fairly long job.

First a male former is carved from wood. Balsa can be used in this case for ease of working as we are not going to beat the living daylight out of it! This time, however, the male mould, as it is known, should be carved exactly to size. Any blisters or excrescences we require can be added at this stage. The whole should now be grain-filled and polished – how well this is done will determine the finish on our glass fibre cowl.

A female mould has now to be cast from plaster of Paris, obtained from a chemist. A suitable cardboard box, or tin, at least $\frac{1}{2}$ in. deeper than the male mould should now be found. The plaster of Paris is mixed with water to a creamy consistency and poured into the mould box. The male mould is now pressed into the liquid plaster of Paris and held there for a few minutes until set. If any tumblehome (i.e. the top of the cowling is narrower than the widest point) is present then the male mould should be slit, vertically, into three pieces to facilitate withdrawal. The male mould is now withdrawn to reveal the female mould in which we lay up our glass fibre cowl. If any air bells are present fill these, and then apply release agent to the mould. I have found that *Vaseline* does this job as well as any of the other proprietary agents.

The glasscloth used for the lay-up should be of the finest weave obtainable. Most grades used for car repairs are far too thick, as is chopped strand mat. The resin used should be of the liquid hardener type. Again the automobile variety with the hardener combined with a filler powder is not suitable as it will not flow through the pores of the glasscloth. Apply a gel coat to the inside of the mould and allow to set before laying up the glasscloth. Two or three layers should be laid up, brushing the resin well in. If tumblehome is present

The nacelle of a Vickers Vimy built by Terry Manley illustrates the good use of 'dirty painted' exhaust pipes. Note also the radiator louvres and authentic plated effect of shim aluminium with embossed rivets.

the mould will have to be broken up to release the cowl, otherwise it can be withdrawn allowing the mould to be used again if needed.

Permanent cowls should be attached to the fuselage with wood screws and epoxy resin adhesive, suitable formers being provided for the attachment.

Detailed portions of cowls can be made from a multitude of materials glued on. For non-stressed parts moulded acetate sheet is very useful. The small fairing at each end of the cylinder blocks of the BE 12b were made in this manner.

Engine details

Dummy engine manufacture is a subject within itself and I can only hope to touch on the major items here.

The fashionable period for complete engine nudity was the 1920s and early 30s when the radial engine dominated the scene. Reproduction of such engines is not as difficult as it first appears but when embarking on such a job, bear in mind that your handiwork in this region is in for a good bashing and the lower 'pots' will be removed every time in a heavy landing. Most engines of the 1914–18 period were either totally enclosed or only partially exposed.

Crankcases are simple – just carve the appropriate shape from balsa and paint accordingly. Cylinders are a little more tricky and, because there are a lot of them, tedious. The simplest method is to smear lengths of the correct-sized dowel with contact adhesive and wind on black insulated electrical wire of the appropriate gauge. The wire should be similarly pre-coated with contact adhesive. Valve gear is simulated with bits of wire, tin and spruce.

Exhaust pipes are best made from thin aluminium tube, stubs being epoxied in place. Bending can usually be performed cold. Open ends can be plugged with wood. Plugs and epoxy are suitably camouflaged by 'dirty painting' – not the pornographic sort but a mixture of dirty pink and black, plastered on thick and rubbed about with the finger until a suitable burnt streaky effect is produced with patches of aluminium showing through. This type of paint application takes a bit of practice. If you are not satisfied with the first attempt wash it off with thinners and have another go. The best effects are obtained by fingering when the dope is almost dry and tears when touched.

Radiators, where applicable, have to be treated strictly on their merits. Some are plain honeycombed, as on the BE, whereas others have an elaborate arrangement of shutters, as on the Vimy. Perhaps the best known shuttered radiator is the Wolseley Viper installation on the SE 5a. The shutters are best made from strips of 1mm ply and laid over the radiator, between the

― DETAIL ―

Exposed radial engines were common up to the 1930s. Replicas can be subject to damage and may also interfere with cooling for the working engine, which happened to this attractive Gloster Gamecock built by Harold Yates.

vertical members, which can be made of the same material. The shutters look best when glued approximately 30 degrees to the horizontal. The radiator itself is of soft balsa, the honeycomb being simulated by means of a hard, sharp-pointed pencil poked in a random fashion over the front surface. If the radiator is not of the shuttered variety then brass gauze makes a neater radiator front at the same time allowing cooling air to pass through to the

Cockpit of John Roth's $\frac{1}{4}$ scale Evans V.P. shows the excellent detail including the exposed instruments above the normal cowl line, inside the windshield, plus radio console. Note, also, the Volkswagen type cylinder heads, specially fabricated in three parts, bolted in place on the Ross twin.

engine. The sides of the radiator should be 'metallised' by one of the methods previously described.

Before embarking on a detailed reproduction of an engine I would recommend, if at all possible, a visit to the aeronautical collection at the Science Museum. In addition to the many aeroplanes on display, there is an extensive collection of aero engines on view. Virtually every British piston engine is represented and quite a few of the prominent foreign types also – two or three photographs of the appropriate engine can save a lot of guesswork.

Scale drawings and photographs of aeroplanes very rarely show, in a manner satisfactory to the modeller, the power plant. Unlike many foreign museums there is usually no restriction whatsoever on photography in any British establishment although a small admission charge may be levied.

Cockpits

The detail work round the nose end of the model has, with one exception, the greatest scope for fine work. The exception, of course, is the cockpit area and it is this region that I will deal with next.

Cockpits can be divided neatly into two categories: open and covered. The majority of subjects which interest the free-flight scale modeller have open cockpits – only in the latter half of the 1930s did military aircraft start to sport the luxury of total enclosure, when speeds and service ceilings had risen to such a level as to make it impossible for flying crew to operate efficiently in fresh air. Civil types with their less hardy occupants were enclosed at a much earlier date, although generally the 'driver' was required to sit in the open until roughly the same date – no doubt a leftover from the horse and carriage era only just past!

A typical 1914–18 war cockpit is shown in the photograph of my BE 12b. Instruments were simple in those days and as there were so few of them (ASI, tachometer, altimeter and compass being the normal complement), they were generally of much larger proportions than on later generations of aeroplanes. Switches were also of huge dimensions, resembling the brass-domed domestic jobs of the era. No semblance of ergonomic layout seems to have been used. Instruments, switches, flare brackets etc., were apparently just chucked into the cockpit in the early days. However, towards the end of the war some degree of order was beginning to be apparent. The SE 5a cockpit looks almost tidy by comparison with its predecessors.

The earliest instruments had black figures on a white background, which are best produced by a sharp pencil on white card. Later instruments had,

—————————— DETAIL ——————————

usually, white figures on a black background which can be reproduced by using white enamel, in a mapping pen, on a black doped card. Enamel is much better than dope for pen use as it is much slower drying – when used for figures on top of a cellulose doped surface it will not leach out the background colour as is always likely to happen when dope is used on top of dope. Never try it the other way around, i.e. dope on top of enamel, as the whole lot will boil up into a horrible mess! All instruments of the WWI period had large bezels. These were made either from aluminium or brass, sometimes painted matt black, and I have found that the best way to produce these is to trepan them from aluminium or brass shims (between .010in. and .020in. thick). For this I use a hand trepanning tool made from an old pair of ink spring bows. The inner limb of the ink pen is removed and the remaining limb sharpened to form a cutting edge – a few spins with this little tool soon cuts a neat circle. Cut the inner circle first, of course. The

Cockpit of my BE 12b illustrates many of the points in the text. Note the very basic 1914–18 period instruments and the flying controls taken straight out of the cockpit. Aluminium framing is used for the windshield, neoprene tubing for the coaming, while the fuselage sides are 'stitched' most realistically.

A 1/12th scale pilot in my Blackburn White Falcon shows the characteristic 'woolly' jacket of 1914. This was made from a substitute chamois leather (unused), which gives a very good 'hairy' effect more akin to a woollen greatcoat used in the early days.

instruments are then formed by gluing the bezel to a disc of celluloid, also produced by the hand trepanner, and then to the figured card. Any type of impact adhesive is suitable for this purpose. If the instruments were flush on the panel, as on the BE, then they can be glued straight on. However, if, as was often the case, the instruments were back mounted, then a disc of balsa will have to be interposed between the card and the panel.

The rest of the cockpit furnishing is a matter of ingenuity with wire, card, dowel and balsa. Watch the weight, though, particularly in rear cockpits of two seaters which are a long way aft of the CG. Seats are best made from card and balsa. The coaming can be reproduced from black neoprene fuel tubing, carefully slit with sharp scissors, and stuck with an impact adhesive over the edges of the cockpit. On larger models, or prototypes where the padding was really thick, thin leather can then be glued over the neoprene tube. I find leather elbow patches sold for patching jackets to be ideal, particularly if salvaged from a jacket that has been worn for at least ten years! In this condition the leather is beautifully supple and will work easily.

Finally, we come to glazing. For an open cockpit this involves nothing more than a windshield. It is worth doing well though, as it is very eye-catching. Painted frames look awful even when new and after a few months' service, when the oil has softened the paint and half of it has disappeared, the effect is even worse. Always frame the shield in thin aluminium. For a simple job like the BE, which is only half framed, light gauge shim can be folded round the edges, with an impact glue applied to both surfaces prior to folding. For more elaborate 'greenhouses', on aeroplanes of later vintage,

— DETAIL —

This view of Terry Manley's RE 8 shows the cockpit and gun positions. The two figures are clad in discarded washleather, with helmets made from leather elbow patches – material is simply stuck to the basic figure with an impact adhesive. The gunner is seen poised for action over his Lewis gun, perched on its movable Scarff ring.

these should be fretted out of light gauge duralumin (aluminium is too soft to fret) and stuck to the outside of the acetate canopy. A simpler method, which is not as durable but infinitely superior to paint, is to cut the frame from thin card, suitably painted, and glue this to the celluloid. Of course, if the canopy possesses double curvature, then this will have to be hot moulded from acetate sheet. Methods of doing this have been described many times in books and magazines.

Pilots

The British Model Flying Association (BMFA) scale rules do not call for a pilot to be seated in the cockpit, and no marks, in fact, are given for such a figure when the model is statically judged. An open cockpit machine, however, looks ridiculous when flown without a pilot. You might just as well leave the wheels off! Certainly, when I am judging scale competitions, in any category, I always mark down the 'appearance in flight' section on all pilotless models. This is a fairly widespread view held by most judges.

Pilots can be carved from balsa, expanded polystyrene, cork etc., moulded from papier maché, acetate, bought ready-made or modified from dolls, plastic kits etc. It matters little from what source he comes, but please fit one. Having obtained your man, again, don't paint him, dress him! A point here –

dress him in the style of the period. Don't forget that up to April 1918 the RFC was part of the Army and the uniform worn was khaki, not RAF blue. This is best reproduced by clothing your man in old washleather. Just cut the washleather into suitable pieces and glue onto the body. Flying helmets are best produced from elbow patching leather; again, cut as necessary.

Guns

Guns are very often poorly reproduced, chiefly, I am sure, because the modeller has not taken the trouble to find out what the original weapons really looked like.

During the 1914–18 conflict, and for a long time afterwards, the major pieces of armoury were the Vickers and Lewis, as used by the Allies, and the Spandau used by the Germans. These are shown at approximately 1/10th scale in Figs 8.8, 8.9 and 8.10 respectively. The Vickers was water-cooled and because of its weight invariably used as a forward-firing fixed gun. The Lewis, being air-cooled and much lighter, was used both as a fixed gun, often mounted above the upper wing, as on the SE 5a and Nieuport, and on the movable Scarff ring as rear cockpit armament on two seaters.

A word or two about reproducing each gun in turn.

(1) **Vickers** The water chest can be made from dowel or round section balsa. The flutes are cut in with a hacksaw. All the rest, with the exception of the metal handle bearers, can be made from balsa. Full-size overall length was $45\frac{1}{2}$ in. (115.5cm) and 'wet weight' 40lbs.

(2) **Lewis** The stock is basically of cruciform section and best made from strip spruce. The barrel fairing is made from dowel or balsa and the barrel end

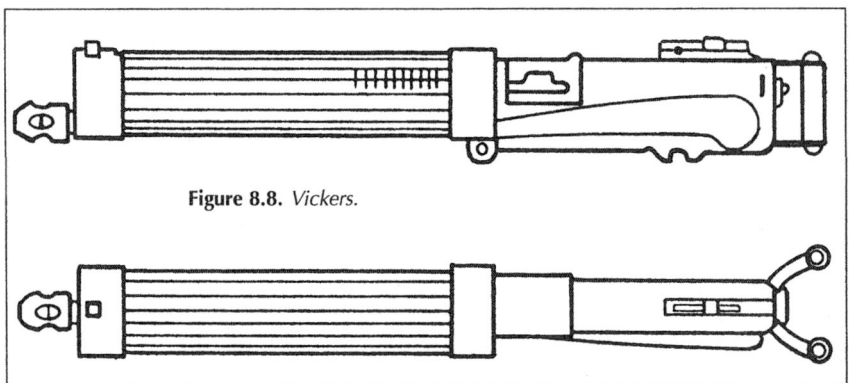

Figure 8.8. *Vickers.*

―――――――――――― DETAIL ――――――――――――

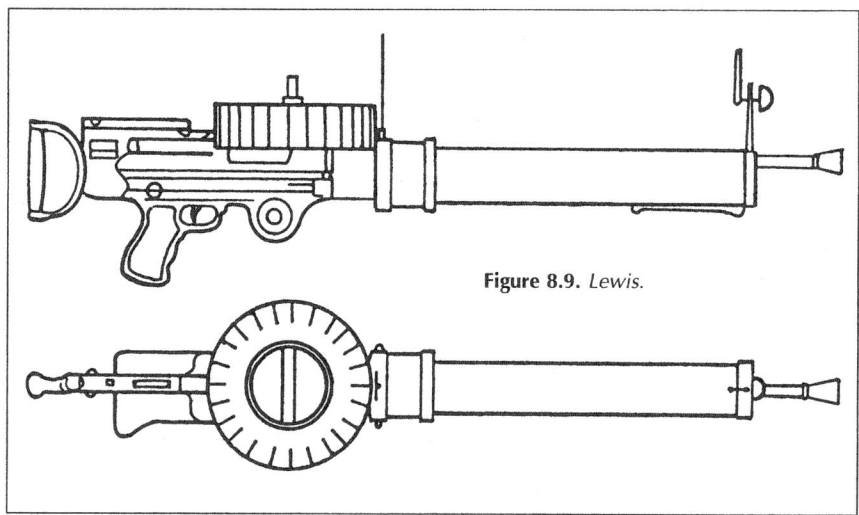

Figure 8.9. *Lewis.*

from brass tube with the end flared. Don't forget to make the slits, along the edges of the ammunition drum, with a hacksaw. These look most effective. The sights are made from wire.

(3) **Spandau** With the exception of the air-cooled barrel surround, the Spandau is produced in a similar manner to the other two guns. The air cooler is a bit of a swine! For small models, 1/12th scale and under, you can paint the cooling slots. Above this scale you have to roll the tube from card in which the slots have been previously cut. Either that or remain patriotic and build aeroplanes with Vickers and Lewises fitted!

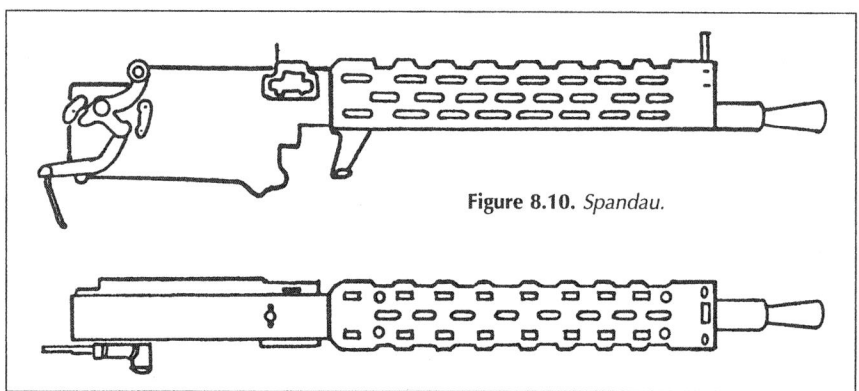

Figure 8.10. *Spandau.*

Undercarriages

Main undercarriage structure was covered in detail in Chapter 4. Tailskids are usually straightforward but just a word about the extended type fitted to the various BE types, the Bristol fighter and the Blackburn White Falcon. Here the five-membered structure is formed from brass tube flattened at the ends and drilled with a $\frac{1}{32}$ in. drill. Wire (20 swg) is then passed through the lower longerons and is soldered to the tubes. A single pin passing through all five members, at their apex, is soldered also. A tinplate fork is soldered to the foot of the centre member, while the skid itself is carved from balsa with tinplate bindings at the central hinge position and upper end. All bindings and the tinplate running sole are epoxied to the skid. Springing is performed by a light rubber band – on simple semi-enclosed skids the skid hinge is simply passed through the lower longerons and the springing band anchored to the upper ones.

Wheels

Until the last few years, there was no alternative but to make replicas of the *Palmer Cord Aerowheels* used almost universally until the 1930s. All model wheels sold were of far too fat a section. In recent years, however, the excellent wheels manufactured by Williams in the US have been available in the UK. Although not perfect, and rather expensive, they are considerably lighter and stronger than anything the average modeller with limited facilities, including a lathe, can produce. For sport flying, I can thoroughly recommend them. For a contest job, however, any model fitted with them will automatically receive a zero for workmanship, and not too many points either for realism from some judges in that particular section.

The biggest problem in home-built wheel manufacture is obtaining the tyre. This must be of rubber or similar elastomer. Believe me, the laminated balsa types shown on the drawings of many scale models are utterly useless on a power model. After three take-offs and one heavy landing the wheels look like something the dog has played with for a week!

The true scale modeller, whenever he sees a ring of rubbery material between $1\frac{1}{2}$ in. and 5in. in diameter promptly acquires it, or preferably two of it. It doesn't matter how it is acquired – begging, borrowing or stealing – it is of far more use to the scale modeller than for its original purpose for which there are bound to be replacements. Unfortunately, 95 per cent of all rings so obtained are the wrong size; invariably the section is too thin. This

———— DETAIL ————

The wheel used on my 1/7th scale SE 5a. The spokes are made from balsa and are then covered with silk and tissue – cutting a hole, of course, for access to the tyre 'valve'! This tyre is from a Hobbies Ltd. wheel, but these regrettably are no longer available.

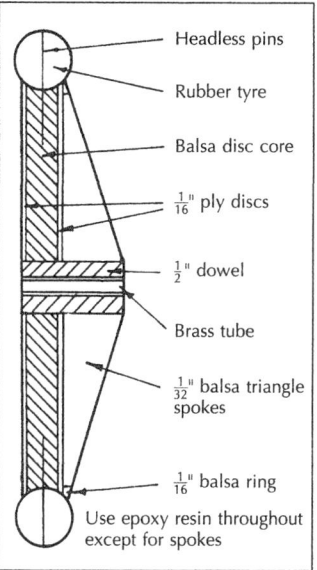

- Headless pins
- Rubber tyre
- Balsa disc core
- $\frac{1}{16}''$ ply discs
- $\frac{1}{2}''$ dowel
- Brass tube
- $\frac{1}{32}''$ balsa triangle spokes
- $\frac{1}{16}''$ balsa ring
- Use epoxy resin throughout except for spokes

Figure 8.11. Section through the wheel.

particularly applies to O rings and Hoover belts, which are only suitable for very early types fitted with glorified bicycle wheels. However, other forms of sealing rings are often larger in section. One source, which alas is no longer available, was the old red metal flanged wheels, fitted with rubber tyres, sold by Hobbies Ltd. The wheels of my SE 5a were made from a pair of these tyres. They are as hard as nails, weigh a ton but at least are the right section and were obtainable in a variety of sizes. I hope someone else markets a similar product shortly. After all, what do all the wooden engine and horse constructors use these days?

Having obtained our tyre, by fair means or foul, we now have to make a wheel to fit round it. This is clearly explained in Fig. 8.11. Having constructed the frame, the 'spokes' are covered in tissue and silk. Before applying the silk, glue an aluminium bezel, produced as per the instruments, onto the tissue and then, after the dope is dry on the silk, cut the valve hole open. The tyre is now glued into place using epoxy adhesive. As I have found no adhesive that will retain a tyre when a heavy model makes a drifting landing, I also poke about eight headless pins through the tyre into the core to assist the glue.

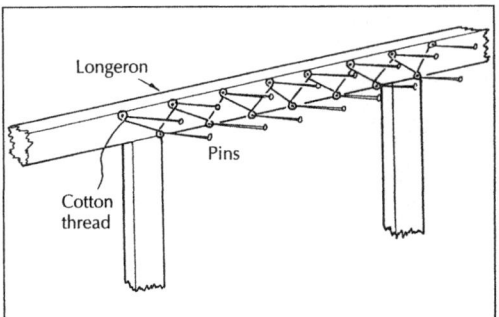

Figure 8.12. *Fabric lacing.*

Fabric lacing

Most fabric-covered aeroplanes have areas where the fabric is laced together to allow areas of the fuselage to be regularly uncovered for routine servicing. During the war years, it would appear that the entire fuselage sides could be stripped on the majority of aeroplanes. In post-war years, a single lacing down the centre line of the belly seemed to be the most popular. It certainly looked neater! Generally, the stitching followed a longeron or cross member. To simulate stitching we therefore stick pins into the longeron or cross member, as per Fig. 8.12. A length of cotton is then tied to the end pin and passed round the pins as shown in Fig. 8.12 and anchored at the end with a blob of cement. Thick dope (100 per cent) is then plastered over the cotton and allowed to dry. The pins are then removed and the final effect should look something like the lacing on the BE. Of course, this operation should be carried out before the final colour doping.

That, apart from the minor points peculiar to each prototype and far too numerous to cover individually, about finishes the detail stage and also the construction of the model.

CHAPTER 9

Flying

You will remember that in Chapter 7 I advocated that trimming should be carried out before the paintwork and details are applied. Some prominent modellers I know scorn such methods and completely finish the model before venturing forth to the flying field. This may be satisfactory for lightly loaded, inherently stable models such as two seaters of the WWI period, but is courting disaster with more heavily loaded models of machines not blessed with so much stability. The one valid objection I can see to trimming an unfinished model is that fuel may soak into the airframe making it difficult to apply the finishing coats. But, taking into consideration that, on average, a dozen power runs of about 30 seconds' duration is all that is required to roughly trim a model (and we are only roughly trimming it at this stage), the

A Sopwith Pup, always a popular subject, makes a characteristic left-hand climb away from the owner's hand. The Old Warden Scale Rally is always a popular meeting, bringing out all the 'fly for fun' enthusiasts, not just the competition fliers.

airframe is not likely to be subjected to fuel over much. In any case, non castor-based diesel fuel will not attack cellulose dope and if the airframe is washed down with neat ether immediately after the trimming session, then no problems of this type will occur. As mentioned in Chapter 7, there are three distinct advantages in trimming a stark unpainted and undetailed model:

(1) The model is much lighter than when completed and, therefore, will fly slower and is less likely to damage itself if, as is very likely, it hits the ground awkwardly.
(2) Any minor, or major, damage is more easily repaired and disguised by the final paint job.
(3) If you write it off or if it just won't fly, you haven't wasted all that time finishing it off!

Pre-flight checks

Before proceeding to the flying field, the model must be given a thorough check out to see if it is fit to fly.

Flying surfaces

View the model from a head-on position and observe for warps – the tail surfaces should be absolutely true to one another. If the sandwich

An unusual subject is the Martinsyde Elephant, chosen here by Vic Driscoll who is well known for his excellent Westland Wapiti.

A photo of me giving the old 'heave-ho' to my faithful Bucker Jüngmann and checking once more that the tail is not warped.

construction method (outlined in Chapter 6) has been followed it is unlikely that the tail surfaces will have warped. However, if a flimsy open framework form of construction has been used then the chances are that the tail *will* have warped, and in that case warps can be eliminated by holding close to an electric fire and twisting the surface in the opposite direction to the warp. With luck the tail may remain true for the trimming session! Almost certainly, warps will have returned before the next flying session and the procedure must be repeated otherwise the flight pattern will have altered for the worse. I cannot emphasise enough the necessity for sound, warp-free tail surfaces – lack of appreciation of this point is the reason for the inconsistent performance of most scale models. If in doubt at this stage it is better to rebuild the tail surfaces before attempting to fly the model. Wing warps are usually not too critical from a trimming point of view on a slow-flying model, and as it is on slow-flying, thin-winged biplanes where they occur most we must be thankful. These warps usually occur very slowly, as the model ages, in a symmetrical pattern, the favourites being washout i.e. tips twisting to give

Terry Manley launches his AW FK 8 on a low-power flight – note the follow-through of the launching arm. (See opposite.)

less incidence, or elliptical dihedral sets in. Apart from being unsightly in any appreciable amount, both add to the lateral stability of the model and can usually be ignored from a basic trimming point of view; provided they are symmetrical that is. If they are asymmetrical then the electric fire must be called into use again.

Hinges to control surfaces

Again as mentioned in Chapter 6, the fishplate type hinges used to attach the rudder and elevators to their respective members should be stiff enough to

Another free flight specialist of long standing is John Palmer, seen attending to his SE 5a in the foreground, while the lesser-known UFAG awaits his attention at the rear.

— FLYING —

 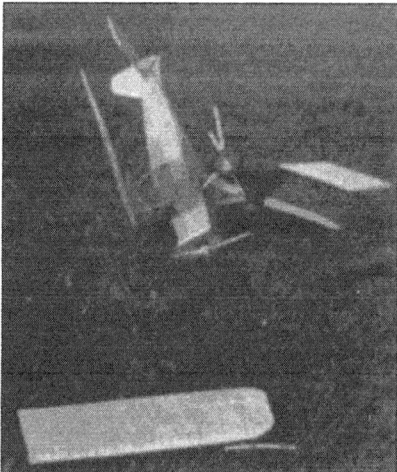

Left, 'Ouch – this is going to HURT!' The FK 8 'arrives' rather hard. Tight right spiral on the glide is due to insufficient right sidethrust to counteract the torque. Right, 'Er, no sir, not quite like that.' My SE 5a in a rather undignified pose having found that terra firma lives up to its name. Although the model looks a mess, no damage resulted thanks to the use of 'knock-off' components. Note the model is unpainted at this stage.

prevent an incidence setting being lost due to their inertia in a heavy landing. It is not possible to make the hinge stiff enough to withstand a direct clout, nor is it desirable to do so, nevertheless they have to be fairly stiff to overcome the inertia loading. Again, if in doubt change them before going to the airfield.

Rigging wires and wing attachments

Check that the wing incidence and dihedral angles are correct and that all wires are tensioned properly and doing their correct amount of work. Do not overtauten the wires, though, otherwise the wing cell will not give in a prang without tearing out all the wire anchorage points.

Check the centre of gravity

Ideally on a scale model the CG should lie somewhere between one-quarter and one-third chord length back from the leading edge on a monoplane, and about half a chord length back from the leading edge of the upper wing of a biplane with an average amount of stagger. If more stagger is present, or the wings are swept back, then due allowance for this must be made when

Charles Essex of the SVAS model section has found a nice patch of long grass at Old Warden – ideal for those trimming flights. Slow-flying models such as his Blackburn Monoplane are a joy to watch, particularly on those calm evenings. Note the prominence of the pilot in an aircraft of this type – certainly an essential feature of the model.

determining the desirable position for the CG. Now balance the model by supporting it, at the desired CG position, by the fingers resting beneath the upper wing just outboard of the centre section. At this stage it is desirable that the model should be nose-heavy and so balance in a nose-down attitude. When the colour dope and details are applied to the tail and rear fuselage it is surprising how much the CG will shift aft. If we have the desirable forward CG apply plasticine to the rear end until the correct balance is achieved. Should the model balance level then almost certainly weight will have to be added to the nose when the model is completed. If it is necessary to add weight to the nose, even in the unpainted condition, then you are in big trouble and you should look immediately into a means by which the back end can be lightened. Having determined where the CG lies, after ballasting if necessary, mark the position with a pencil.

First engine run

Never leave this until you arrive on the field, as with a fully cowled motor there are bound to be little problems with fuel feed, cooling or control adjustment etc. Replacing the cowling when the engine is running can be tricky at first. Get yourself fully familiar with operating the engine, particularly at low revs, and check the fuel consumption so that you know at what level the fuel should be in the tank for runs of 10 seconds, 20 seconds, 30 seconds, 1 minute etc. A transparent tank is essential of course. Be completely happy about the motor before attempting to trim – you will have enough to bother you in getting the brute to fly without letting an awkward engine set-up annoy you! When you start worrying about the motor you start to do foolish things like throwing the model in the air as soon as it starts without thinking properly, which is how 90 per cent of trimming prangs occur.

Initial test glides

For the initial glide trimming, long grass is necessary – 9 inches long minimum, 18 inches long ideal. Generally most service airfields are kept cut pretty short and you should look elsewhere for the initial glides. A large field is unnecessary; a 50-yard square will do at a pinch although a bit longer is desirable. Overgrown wasteground is ideal although check that there aren't any old motorbikes, bathtubs etc. concealed in it before you dash your pride and joy to destruction!

Now wait until it is flat calm or at least less than 4 mph. You may have to be patient for several weeks for this, particularly in the early part of the year. September or October are usually the best months for trimming scale models. Winds tend to be at their minimum in the early morning or late evening, when the grass is at its wettest! When conditions are right, launch the model in a slightly nose-down attitude into wind (if there is any) and observe the

Rather more successful flight by the ETA 15 powered, 1/7th scale SE 5a, thanks to the model now being fully trimmed and finished. It has just taken off from the runway and is making a characteristic left-hand climbing turn.

glide. Try to launch with a long sweeping arm action, accelerating the model all the time so that it just flies out of your hand. If you throw too hard you will stall it, while if you do not throw hard enough the model will fall short into the grass. Try to keep the wings parallel to the ground at the moment of release – you should aim for a straight flat glide without any tendency for a wing to drop. Unless the model is obviously violently out of trim, repeat the glide about six times to check that the pattern is consistent and any stalling tendency is not due to incorrect launching. If the model is definitely stalling, and this is the most common condition at this stage, remove a little plasticine from the tail if the CG is in a reasonably aft position. If this is not possible then depress the elevators very slightly – $\frac{1}{16}$ in. at a time is sufficient. Check this with a straight edge and rule. If the model is gliding too steeply, then the opposite treatment can be given. A word of warning here: although biplanes can be made to glide quite flat, they sink at a fairly high rate due to the high drag of the bracing wires, so do not mistake sink for a steep glide. Turns can be straightened out by judicious application of opposite rudder. Do not be confused by a stall though – very often a wing will drop in a stall. Cure the stall before attempting to straighten the direction. If the model is out of trim the grass will prevent serious damage during these initial tests, but there is one drawback however – it tends to snag up flying wires and if any fly off in a heavy landing it is the devil's own job to find them again. When picking the model up develop the habit of giving it the once-over to make sure everything

The Bristol Monoplane Scout is a popular Nexus plan (FSP 759) and has a span of 46in. taking engines up to 1.5cc. This excellent version appeared at the 1971 All-Scale Rally at Old Warden.

Beautifully constructed 1/12th scale version of the Westland Wapiti by Vic Driscoll is 46in. span and uses ME Snipe for power. The model had not flown when this picture was taken at Old Warden. Vic has recently (1997) built a second version of this aircraft.

is there, because if you have left the spot you will never find it again! Continue this habit even when flying over short grass and train your 'fetcher mites' too, otherwise collect it yourself.

Before proceeding to the power stage, have a thorough examination of the model again and check that nothing has shifted or is working loose. The cabane should be examined closely at this time for signs of strain, then record in a notebook the exact settings of the rudder and elevators.

If the long-grassed field is large enough, you can proceed immediately on to the first power flights. If not, transfer to the flying field and power trim as soon as weather conditions permit.

Power trimming

Start the engine and run it about one-quarter full power, and let it run for about two minutes to warm up. If you neglect this the engine may speed up after launching with disastrous results. Launch as before with about 20 seconds of fuel left – an extended powered glide should result, preferably with a slight left turn. If a slight *right* turn is evident, the flight path should be straightened by a slight application of left rudder. Increase the power for the next flight so that the model just loses height under power; any slight stalling tendency can be corrected with a small amount of down elevator. As the power is increased, the tendency to turn left is more pronounced and right rudder may be required to correct. Check that the glide turn to the right,

SCALE AIRCRAFT FOR FREE FLIGHT

Photographed against the sun, a Bristol Bullet displays its structure. The Nexus Plans Service plan FSR 226 for a 37in. model was primarily designed by Eddie Riding as a rubber-powered model, but the plan includes detail of conversion for 1cc engines.

which will almost certainly ensue, is not getting too tight or a spiral-in on glide will result when the engine stops.

If, as power is increased, the left turn cannot be corrected by right rudder then flying must cease immediately and the model taken back to the workshop for more right sidethrust to be applied. If, as recommended in Chapter 4, the engine is mounted on a plate then it is a relatively simple matter to make

The Fairchild P2 makes an excellent introduction to scale modelling as it has simple lines, an easily reproduced engine and high wing layout for good stability. This example is Enya 15D powered, and was made by J. Archbold of Leicester.

This picture illustrates the simplicity of changing thrust lines on models by using the engine plate mounting method. The Mills 1.3 c.c. is shown with the new and old engine plates (which were used to reduce the right-thrust by 2 degrees) on the DH 9A – the easily-accessible nose of which is clearly visible.

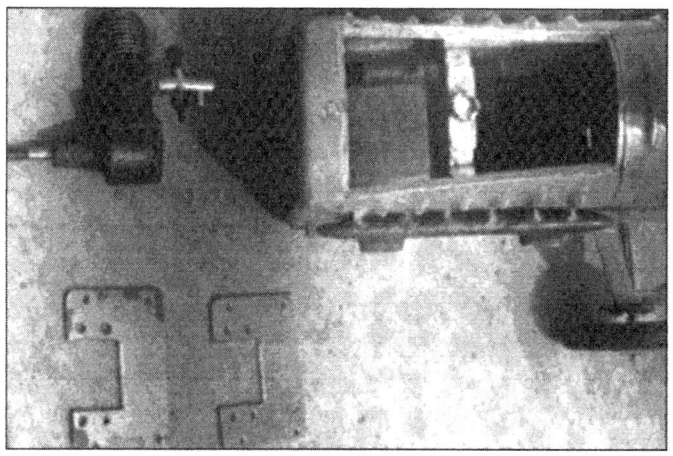

another plate with more sidethrust, displacing the engine sideways to allow the crankshaft to emerge from the same hole in the cowling. Do not attempt to continue flying by correcting the left turn with a lot of right rudder

Left: A flashback to the 1960 British Nationals shows R. Hackett, of Chichester, kneeling with his $\frac{1}{6}$ th scale Bucker Jüngmeister finished in Swiss markings, and John Simmance with a $\frac{1}{8}$ th scale Sopwith Snipe in the R.A.A.F. colour scheme. The Jüngmeister has Frog 80 power, the Snipe a Frog 150R.

Eric's Rumpler CIV was an extremely attractive ship, but one which he placed in his 'No. 2' category – better suited to those with prior, scale modelling experience, but it was still quite a stable flier.

otherwise a smash is bound to occur. At this stage in the proceedings, you must be prepared to see the model take a few bashes, but if it has been built on the flexible principles outlined in previous chapters, and is reasonably light, the worst that will happen is as shown in the photograph on page 105 of the SE 5a taken during a trimming session. Everything was back together and the model rerigged within 20 minutes, without any damage occurring.

Very often as power is increased, a stalling tendency develops which cannot be corrected by down elevator without steepening the glide too much. More downthrust is the answer here, best applied by packing washers between the rear engine lugs and the mounting plate.

After about a dozen flights, and much diligent adjustment, you should achieve a wide shallow left-hand climbing turn, followed by a flat glide with a wide turn either to the left or right. Never allow the model to turn right under power in any circumstances! A pile-in is the almost certain result. Some very stable machines like the BE 12b and the Jüngmann will take a very wide right turn on low power, but the tendency of the gyrocouple to stick the nose into the floor is always there. Never take any chances – always trim left on power.

When you are satisfied with the trim from a hand-launch you can try a take-off from the runway, if your airfield is blessed with such a luxury. Make sure the engine is giving sufficient power for a reasonable climb and there is at least 30 seconds worth of fuel in the tank before releasing. Nothing is more disastrous than the engine cutting on the climb-out about 5ft above a hard runway! Face the model so that the wind is coming on at about 15 degrees from the left, *not* straight into it. When the model is released, not pushed in any way, it should swing left about this amount before gaining directional stability and so be pointing into wind at the moment of take-off. Only practical experience with the model will determine the actual amount if swing, but 15 degrees is about average.

Some prototypes take off better than others, and some I am afraid, are very loth to do so at all. It is very difficult to pinpoint what governs take-off performance; ideally the model should swing slightly to the left on the initial acceleration, due to torque reaction, then as the tail surfaces gain aerodynamic power, the model should run straight for a few yards before lifting both wheels off simultaneously, followed by a straight climb before commencing the left turn. Prototypes with forward disposed undercarriages, which are fine for preventing a nose-over on landing, are prone to 'waltzing' on the runway before take-off – if they ever manage it. WWI single seaters tend to come into this category. Aeroplanes with low-set undercarriages, just in front of the CG such as WWI two seaters, are generally much better performers of the take-off manoeuvre, while good suspension and free-running wheels (oil them with a drop of fuel) are a big asset to a clean take-off. Lightly loaded models are often worse at taking off than a heavier machine (within moderation that is) providing sufficient power is available. The reason for this is that the model has more forward speed and hence directional stability, from the tail, before the lift effects from the wings take charge of things. Very often, angling the undercarriage so that one wheel leads in the direction of the turn helps cure a wayward take-off tendency.

Once you have determined that the model will take-off and produce a reasonable flight pattern, or come to the conclusion that take-offs are impossible and it is to be a hand-launch only model, pack up flying immediately

Floatplanes are an unusual choice, but do make attractive subjects – at least they won't nose-over when landing on short grass! Note the alternative undercarriage in the foreground. This example of a Piper Cub was built by E. Wisbey and uses a Frog 3.49D to carry its $4\frac{1}{2}$ lb aloft.

That fellow Manley again – this time giving a decisive launch to his R.E.8 – not the sort of aircraft to gently float from your hands! Still going strong, Terry was placed third in the 1997 Scale Nationals, flying a $1\frac{1}{2}$ Strutter.

and wash it down with ether. Do not be tempted to continue flying – you may only damage it and nothing further is to be gained, for a certain amount of retrimming is bound to be necessary when the model emerges in its completed and heavier state.

Before taking the model home record in a notebook (a separate logbook for each model is useful – I tend to use the folio containing information presented to the judges) the following:

(1) Port and starboard elevator settings. Place a straight edge along the top, or bottom, of a certain tailplane rib and measure the amount of droop, or rise, of each elevator between the straight edge and the centre line of the trailing edge.
(2) Rudder setting – left or right in a similar manner.
(3) Measure the CG position from the leading edge of the centre section.
(4) Make a note of any warps that are in the wings.
(5) Record propeller size, approximate amount of power for a normal flight and the amount of fuel required for a 30-second engine run.

Do not wait until you get the model home before doing this as you may knock the tail surfaces in transit so destroying your whole evening's work.

* * *

The foregoing covers the initial stages of trimming the model which I consider best accomplished while the model is in an unpainted state. When the model emerges from its final trimming session it should be complete in every detail. In its finished condition it will, of course, be several ounces heavier than when it last flew, and will therefore fly somewhat faster when gliding and under power. It will also be somewhat more vulnerable to damage; especially

Pioneer aircraft often form the subject for rubber-driven or small-engined power models, as this example seen on a windy All-Scale day at Old Warden in 1971. Those small tail surfaces must give the owner difficulty in getting the right trim!

with regard to detail work. However, we are armed with the knowledge that the beast *will* fly and is unlikely to strike the ground with a sickening thud on its first flight.

Final trimming flights

Again as outlined previously, carry out a thorough pre-flight check on the model before proceeding to the field. Check all surfaces for warps – there should be none in the tail surfaces. Any warps in the wings should correspond to those on the previous outing; reference to the logbook should verify this. Set the control surfaces exactly to the positions recorded during the initial test flights and bring the CG back to exactly the position also recorded, by either removing ballast from the tail (if you are lucky) or adding

Gene Lapansie, of Michigan, is certainly a monster F/F scale enthusiast – here he cowers beneath his Berliner Joyce, powered by an Arden 19.

weight to the nose (if you aren't). Do *not* attempt to fly with the CG further aft than previously, even if you have to stuff three ounces of lead in the nose. Finally, run the engine up again to check that the jet is not blocked with paint, and everything functions as before.

If the long grass is still handy it is worth having a few hand-glides over it to check that the trim is basically the same. Minor correction to the elevators is in order at this time, but do not touch the rudder before the first power flight. I do not recommend a test glide over short grass as this can do more harm than good. Very little is to be gained from hand-glides once the model is in reasonable trim.

Start the motor to give sufficient power for a long powered glide, allowing it to warm thoroughly before hand-launching over grass well away from the runway. Make sure there is enough fuel for at least 20 seconds run. Observe that the flight pattern appears to be following a slight turn to the left or straight ahead – if there is any tendency to turn to the right apply a little left rudder, while similarly any slight stalling tendency can be damped out with a little down elevator. Slowly increase power and by very small adjustments of the tail surfaces, trim for optimum power and glide performance. This can take a considerable time, but do not be satisfied with a tight left climbing turn and a tight turn on the glide. Aim for a wide shallow left-hand climb and a very wide circling glide, even if it means making yet another engine mounting plate to get the engine thrust line/rudder combination correct. Some models,

There were many pre-war kits for rubber-driven scale models of high quality. Among them is this Hawker Demon by Keelbild, which Doug McHard has made to his own inimitable standards. Those ailerons are painted on with airbrush effect.

A typical scene at an Aeromodeller All-Scale Rally at Old Warden is this launch of a Bucker Jüngmeister. Modellers usually choose to make the in-line engine version as Nexus Plans Service plan FSP 807X, but in this instance the blistered radial cowling is well represented.

the Jüngmann being a good example, possess weathercock stability on the glide. If trimmed with only a very slight glide turn and the engine cuts with the model's head within 45 degrees into wind, it will weathercock all the way down. With experience it is surprising how often this flight pattern can be repeated. If there is a breeze blowing it confers a double advantage: (a) you don't have far to walk for it and (b) the landing speed, relative to the ground, is very much reduced.

A word now about propellers and developed engine power. It is most noticeable how much more power the fully finished model requires to fly it compared to when the initial trimming was carried out in a 'stark' condition. In fact, if you are a bit marginal on engine size and you have laid the paint and detail work on with a trowel, you may find that the engine is hard put to develop sufficient power to fly.

Now, the propeller which seems to extract the most power from an engine on a test bench will not necessarily be the best for the model. A Mills .75 will give its best output on a 7in. × 4in., but if the cowling of the model is 5in. diameter, the 1in. of blade sticking outside the periphery is not going to be much good, is it? Here the long-stroke Mills comes into its own for it will turn a 9in. × 4in. or 10in. × 3in. quite happily, developing far more usable power in the model than with the 7in. × 4in. This is, of course, what makes the modern .049 glow motor so useless for scale work – offered 10in. × 3in. it wouldn't be capable of turning it fast enough to keep the plug warm! Similarly, the Mills 1.3 develops most power on a 9in. × 4in. but will swing a

SCALE AIRCRAFT FOR FREE FLIGHT

Judges at work inspecting a club scale competition in the heyday of the Blackburn A/C club at Brough in 1966.

12in. × 4in. or even a 12in. × 6in. if you want it to. The power output at 2,000 rpm isn't too good though! Generally a 1.3 in a two seater of about 45in.–50in. span performs best on a 10in. × 4in. or 10in. × 6in. Quite often we don't want the full power from the engine for realistic flight so it is, therefore, better to load up the engine with a coarser pitch propeller than running it under-compressed. In the latter condition there is always the danger of the engine gaining power as it heats up, and it is not a very pleasant sight to see your pride and joy turning in a tight left bank with the wing tip 6 inches above the tarmac. However, it is surprising how many scale models will hold height in this attitude. The reason for it is that, unlike a turn to the right, the gyrocouple is dragging the nose up all the time while the torque reaction is digging the wing in.

When changing propeller sizes beware of the trim change that will occur due to the change in torque reaction. The more torque the engine develops the greater will be the tendency to turn left. As stated previously, this is usually safe; the danger lies when you change to a propeller with less torque reaction and the model turns right.

For all trimming flights use a nylon propeller but once you have got the model flying consistently, change to a wooden one. It looks so much more realistic on the model both when the engine is stationary and running.

Once the model is trimmed it is worth locking the elevator settings with balsa cement blobs in the hinge groove. However, when it has set check that shrinkage has not altered the setting – I do not think it worthwhile locking the rudder setting as this item gets a lot of bumps during nose-overs and it is better if it moves. Before *every* flight, measure the rudder setting with a rule and straight edge. It is a small chore, but if carried out is likely to lengthen the flying life of the model tenfold.

Contest flying

If you intend to enter the model in contests it is advisable to limit the amount of flying the model does during its contest life. When the model is trimmed to perfection, and this can involve maybe 30 or 40 flights, I would recommend only making a couple of test flights, to check the trim, prior to each contest. Although free-flight scale contests are not as well supported as they used to be (entries of 25 were not unknown in the 1950s and early 60s), quite a number are still held making it worthwhile building a model with which to do the 'rounds'.

Like any other contest flying, it is essential to be organised. Two essentials are required to enter a free-flight scale competition:
(1) a well trimmed model and
(2) scale documentation.

An immaculate specimen of a model is not essential – indeed I have seen many a contest won with a well-trimmed model that was far from perfect

This photo of the Shuttleworth Collection's Bristol Fighter shows fabric lacing and the different appearance of fabric and metal areas, as well as lots of other detail. Could be included with scale documentation, but most important are views of the complete aircraft, at least one of which should be in colour.

whereas the immaculate job which has "I have never flown" written all over it has pranged at the first attempt. All models must fly for at least 30 seconds to qualify and, as about 40 per cent of the total marks can be obtained for the flying performance, it can be seen that the flying is of paramount importance. If documentation is not presented to the judges then your model cannot be judged for scale appearance. Kind judges may give you marks for workmanship but it is unlikely you will overcome the opposition – unless yours is the only model to fly! Therefore a good folio is essential, and this should be presented in the form of a folder containing, as a minimum:

An accurate scale drawing of the subject to a minimum of 1/72 scale.

Three photographs of the subject aircraft, at least one of which should be in the colour scheme and markings of the model reproduced.

Extra photographs showing details of the aircraft can be presented, and indeed are desirable, but do not overdo it and confuse the judges. Remember, their time is strictly limited and there may be a lot of aeroplanes to judge.

You have two attempts to make each of the two competition flights. The highest flight score is aggregated to the scale and workmanship points, therefore you have in effect four attempts to make a flight of 30 seconds – not very difficult. At each attempt you have a maximum of 3 minutes to get airborne, and if the flight does not last 30 seconds then it is classed as an attempt. If you know that the model is capable of taking off, you should

Being assisted by master modeller Cesare Milani as I wind my rubber-powered Hurricane in one of the Cardington airship hangars.

One of Doug McHard's masterpieces, this $\frac{1}{24}$ scale D.H.2 for CO_2 power is only 14in. (355mm) span and weighs exactly 1oz. The tank is in the nose.

always attempt a rise off the ground (ROG) at the first attempt. If it fails to do so, hand-launch the model at the second attempt and record a score. Both attempts of the second flight then can be made as an ROG. As the take-off

Another picture of Doug McHard's DH2. The Brown Junior CO_2's cylinder blends in perfectly with the dummy pots (it's mounted inverted, if you couldn't spot it!). Note the beautifully carved prop, which is to scale and yet fine for flying, and the intricate bracing.

It can happen to even top experts! Terry Manley's Blackburn 1912 Monoplane chose an unsuitable landing place with the unfortunate result shown here.

accounts for something like 10 per cent of the total marks it is essential that the manoeuvre is scored at all costs. Many a contest has been lost due to an ineffective take-off performance.

The appearance of the model in flight is assessed, as is the glide and approach to landing. The actual landing is not marked as the model invariably tips up – it is pure luck if the model happens to land into wind on a runway. Time spent trimming to get the flight pattern attractive will pay off when the flight is being marked. A low flying speed, if appropriate, is also well received.

Above all in contest flying, do not get harassed. You have plenty of time and attempts, so if you fail at the first, sit back and take stock of the situation, religiously check all the control surface settings and let the engine cool off before you try again.

The serious contest modeller has horses for courses. The biggest enemy of the free-flight scale model is wind. On a calm day the large slow-flying model is the most impressive, but on a windy day it can be a bit of a handful, particularly at take-off. A smaller, more heavily loaded model, such as the Nimrod, is a better bet in such conditions as its faster flying speed enables it to 'punch' the headwind better and it is not so upset by gusts. The smaller model is also less likely to be damaged during fast downwind landings. I have seen lightly loaded models flown in windy conditions, but it is usually prudent to hand-launch. I won the 1968 Super Scale trophy with the SE 5a flown in a 20-knot wind – only one other competitor managed to get airborne.

Properly trimmed, a good scale model will fly in quite severe winds; it is the landings which are the tricky part. It is just luck whether you touch down at 0 mph into wind, or 40 mph downwind. Flying in such conditions is not much fun, but worth the risk in competitions, especially if you use an old model.

My output is about one free-flight model per year, but I do build other models I hasten to add. I try to have it trimmed out by April, or early May at the latest, in good time for the Super at the Nationals. It is then kept solely for contest work for the remainder of the season. However, if the next year's model turns out to be not so good, then it may have to last for two seasons of contest flying. If the new model is OK then it becomes a reserve and is flown quite a reasonable amount as a sport model but still kept looking fairly decent in case of need. By its third season it is used purely as a sport model. After that it is living on borrowed time! Four to five years is about the average lifespan for one of my scale models although some have managed as much as seven. The SE 5a took on a new lease of life after 'retirement' with radio and an OS 30.

It can happen to even top experts (2)! The effects of many seasons of seeping diesel fuel are shown in the demise of my Rumpler CV, after a wing collapsed in flight. Plenty of fuel-proofer round the engine bay helps delay this type of horror.

Glossary

Most of the terms used in this book are likely to be known to the reader or are explained by the text, but there are some which may require definition. The following list also includes examples of general model aircraft terms which may not be really familiar.

Aerofoil A lifting surface also used as an abbreviated form of 'aerofoil section'. US usage 'airfoil'.
Aerotow Towing of a glider to release height by a powered aircraft.
Aileron Movable control surface on trailing edge of wing, usually at the tip but occasionally inset and sometimes extending along most of the trailing edge.
Airbrakes Extendable panels (sometimes rotatable e.g. undercarriage fairings) to increase aircraft drag and produce deceleration.
Angle of attack The angle at which an aerofoil meets the air (not related to any structure).
Angle of incidence The angle at which an aerofoil (wing or tailplane etc.) is mounted on the airframe relative to a common datum line.
Balsa Naturally light weight tropical hardwood.
Banana oil A form of cellulose lacquer.
Bay The area of biplane wings between sets of interplane struts.
Bellcrank A pivoted component, often metal, with holes at 90 degrees converting a force applied into a movement at 90 degrees to the force.
BMFA British Model Flying Association (formerly the SMAE, Society of Model Aeronautical Engineers).
Bulkhead A main fuselage cross-member, usually solid as opposed to a frame, sited at a point of stress or loading.
Bungee Cotton-covered multi-strand elastic rope.
Cabane The structure of struts and bracing wires on which a wing is mounted above the fuselage.
Camber The curvature of a cross-section, especially of an aerofoil.
Canard Form of aircraft using a noseplane or stabiliser ahead of the wing instead of the more conventional rear-mounted tailplane.
Cantilever Without external support e.g. a wing which has no struts or visible bracing.
Capping Thin, narrow strip of wood set on top and/or bottom of a rib to form a T or I section.
Centre-section A short, flat middle portion of a wing structure most often used for mounting wings to fuselages. On parasol wings may include main fuel tank etc.
CG Centre of Gravity, the point through which all of an aircraft's weight may be considered to act, i.e. the balance point.
Chord The fore and aft width of an aerofoil.
Chuck glider A hand-thrown glider usually of solid sheet balsa construction.
CL Centre of Lift.
CLA Centre of Lateral Area.
Clevis A forked connector with a pin on one side, sprung into place.
Closed loop A control linkage of two lines exerting a pull for movement either way about a pivot line.
Cockpit The pilot's position in an aircraft.
Collet Stub of thick-walled tube with a grub-screw through the wall.
Compressed air engine Form of motor running on a supply of air pumped into a reservoir tank.
CO_2 motor Form of motor running on a supply of carbon dioxide gas. Can be minute – down to $1\frac{1}{2}$ mm bore and stroke.
Crutch A strong shallow frame forming a base for a fuselage built with formers and stringers.
Crystal Slice of quartz vibrating at a constant frequency controlling a radio signal.
Decalage The difference in angles of incidence between the upper and lower wings of a biplane etc.
Delta Of triangular shape.
Dethermaliser Device for spoiling a model's trim to produce rapid but safe descent, usually fuse or clockwork timer operated.

GLOSSARY

Diesel Compression-ignition engine working on a two-stroke principle.
Dihedral The slight V angle of a wing seen from ahead. If it is inverted it is anhedral, if more than a central change of angle it is polyhedral.
Dope Nitrate or butyrate cellulose preparation used for tautening and/or airproofing covering. Also used as an adhesive for tissue etc. and colour variants are available.
Dowel Strip of close-grained wood (usually birch) machined to circular cross-section.
Elevator Movable control surface attached to horizontal tailplane.
Elevon Control surface combining movements of both elevators and ailerons, generally on tail-less aircraft.
Fin Fixed vertical surface conventionally at the rear of the aircraft with the rudder hinged to it.
Flaps Movable surfaces at the wing trailing edge to steepen the glide and increase lift at low speeds.
Former Light structural member to support stringers producing shape required.
Freewheel Ability of propeller to disengage from drive and 'windmill' freely, usually employed on rubber-powered models.
Frequency Cycles per second of oscillations (of radio waves etc.).
Fuselage Main structural member of aircraft, mounting wings, tail, engine etc. in appropriate relationship and having space within for crew, equipment etc.
Geodetic Construction of curved surfaces with short omnidirectional structural members.
Glowplug Similar to a sparking plug but has electrodes connected by a fine coil of wire (nichrome or similar) which glows on $1\frac{1}{2}$ or 2 volts for starting but thereafter retains heat from fuel combustion sufficiently to ignite following charge.
Gyrocouple The nose-up or nose-down force created by gyroscopic precession in flight, the propeller acting as a gyroscope.
Hardwood Timber from a deciduous tree, botanically, but in modelling any wood hard in characteristics.
Horn Small projection to which a control rod or cable is attached to operate a moving surface.
Jig A rigid support for accurate construction and/or repetition of a component.
Lacing The continuous cord and eyelet system used to secure removable fabric panels in place.
Leading edge (l.e.) The forward extremity of a wing etc. or the structural spar at the front of a wing, tailplane, fin etc.
Longeron A main fore and aft member of a basic fuselage structure.
Longitudinal dihedral Sometimes used in modelling to express the difference in incidence between wing(s) and tailplane.
Methanol Methyl alcohol, a component of glowplug fuel.
Moment The product of a force and the distance at which it is applied from the rotational point, but also used as an abbreviation for 'moment arm' which is simply the distance element.
Monocoque A shape (e.g. a fuselage) in which all stresses etc. are carried by a skin with minimum internal structure.
Nacelle Engine housing(s) separate from main fuselage, also used for early fuselages with pusher airscrews.
Ornithopter Aircraft using flapping wings for power flight.
Parasol Wing position spaced above the fuselage.
Peanut Rubber-powered scale flying model of up to 13in. maximum wingspan.
Petrol engine Internal combustion engine employing spark ignition, normally using petrol (gasoline) for fuel.
Piano wire Hard spring steel wire, often plated or polished.
Pistachio Miniature rubber-powered scale flying model not exceeding 8in. span, usually flown indoors.
Pitch Distance moved forward by a propeller (or screw) in one revolution. Also the rotation of an aircraft about its lateral axis.
Prang Slang (originally RAF) for a crash.
Precession The reaction of a gyroscope at 90 degrees to a force applied; this and rigidity in space are the two characteristics peculiar to gyroscopic rotation.
Profile Normally a shape seen for the side but in this text a reference to Profile Publications, a range of detailed booklets on specific aircraft available when the series of article was written.
PSS Power Scale Slope – engine-less scale aircraft used in slope soaring.
Pylon A member carrying a wing, in the form of a solid structure rather than a cabane.
Rib Fore and aft member giving shape to a wing or tail.

SCALE AIRCRAFT FOR FREE FLIGHT

Rib tapes Narrow strips of fabric along rib lines covering stitching of surface material to each rib.
Riblet Short rib or ribs sited between full ribs, usually extending from the leading edge to the front spar. The purpose is to prevent covering sag in the important first 10–15 per cent of the wing surface, for aerodynamic reasons. Also strengthens the leading edge.
Roll Rotation of aircraft about the longitudinal axis.
Rudder Vertical movable surface influencing the direction of travel, rate of turn etc.
Sanding sealer Cellulose-based fluid containing filler powder (talc or clay) for filling wood grain etc.
Scale Reproduction of an object in a different size, usually reduced in the case of aircraft.
Scantlings The cross-sectional dimensions of materials from which parts of a structure are made.
Shirring elastic Thin cotton-covered elastic thread available from haberdashery sources.
Slat A small, lightly sprung-loaded strip of metal mounted close to the leading edge at a wing tip. Normally flush to the wing surface, it lifts as the wing approaches stalling point, influencing the airflow and delaying tip stall.
Slot A narrow aperture through the wing, usually near the tip, parallel with the leading edge, allowing air to flow through from beneath the wing to delay airflow breakdown near the stalling angle and hence to delay the stall.
Solid scale Expression used to identify non-flying scale models, originally carved but now often employing plastics etc.
Spacer Vertical or horizontal member between longerons.
Span Distance between extreme tips of wings or tailplane.
Spar A main structural member, usually extending through wing or tailplane.
Spark ignition Firing of fuel/air mixture in cylinder by means of an electric spark.
Spin Rotational descent of aircraft in which wings are in fully stalled condition and speed of descent constant.
Spiral Descent of an aircraft in a spiral path, normally with increasing speed.
Spoilers Devices to increase drag and reduce lift to facilitate losing height and landing.
Spruce Springy hard wood used for spars etc. having greater strength (but also greater weight) than balsa.
Stabiliser Customarily used in the USA for 'tailplane'.
Stagger The positioning of one wing forward or aft of the other on a biplane etc.
Stall Loss of lift occasioned by breakdown of airflow over wing surfaces.
Stick Slang term for control column.
Stringer Light structural fore and aft member giving shape to a fuselage.
Sweepback Angling of wing halves from a lateral straight line with tips aft of root. (Rare opposite is sweepforward.)
Template A pattern for marking or cutting round.
Thermal Warm air bubbles forming a rising current due to unequal heat reflection of ground surfaces. Rising air is, of course, balanced by areas of sink as cooler air descends.
Thrust The propulsive force produced by the turning propeller.
Torque The tendency of the aircraft to rotate in the opposite direction to the propeller, caused by air resistance to the propeller's movement.
Torsion bar A part of a structure which absorbs stresses by twist in a length of (usually) piano wire.
Trailing edge (t.e.) The rear edge of a wing etc. or the structural member forming it. (On some early aircraft the t.e. was a wire which, when the covering tightened, produced a characteristic scalloped effect.)
Trim The balance of forces acting on an aircraft which must be achieved for stable flight.
Turnbuckle A double-ended left-hand/right-hand threaded adjuster used to tighten wires. Sometimes termed a 'bottlescrew'.
Undercamber The concavity of the underside of a wing etc.
Undercarriage The wheels and strut arrangement comprising the equipment needed to take off and land, absorb landing shocks etc.
Wash-in The increase of the angle of incidence towards the wing tip produced by a warp in the structure (which may or may not be deliberate!).
Wash-out The decrease of the angle of incidence towards the wing tip (which is normally much safer for model flying than wash-in).
Yaw Rotation of the aircraft about its vertical axis.